Adolescent Social Behavior and Health

Charles E. Irwin, Jr., *Editor*
University of California, San Francisco

NEW DIRECTIONS FOR CHILD DEVELOPMENT
WILLIAM DAMON, *Editor-in-Chief*
Clark University

Number 37, Fall 1987

Paperback sourcebooks in
The Jossey-Bass Social and Behavioral Sciences Series

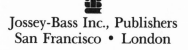

Jossey-Bass Inc., Publishers
San Francisco • London

Charles E. Irwin, Jr. (ed.).
Adolescent Social Behavior and Health.
New Directions for Child Development, no. 37.
San Francisco: Jossey-Bass, 1987.

New Directions for Child Development
William Damon, *Editor-in-Chief*

New Directions for Child Development is published quarterly by
Jossey-Bass Inc., Publishers (publication number USPS 494-090).
Second-class postage paid at San Francisco, California, and at
additional mailing offices. POSTMASTER: Send address changes to
Jossey-Bass Inc., Publishers, 433 California Street, San Francisco,
California 94104.

Editorial correspondence should be sent to the Editor-in-Chief,
William Damon, Department of Psychology, Clark University,
Worcester, Massachusetts 01610.

Library of Congress Catalog Card Number LC 85-644581

International Standard Serial Number ISSN 0195-2269

International Standard Book Number ISBN 1-55542-939-4

Cover art by WILLI BAUM

Manufactured in the United States of America

Ordering Information

The paperback sourcebooks listed below are published quarterly and can be ordered either by subscription or single copy.

Subscriptions cost $52.00 per year for institutions, agencies, and libraries. Individuals can subscribe at the special rate of $39.00 per year *if payment is by personal check.* (Note that the full rate of $52.00 applies if payment is by institutional check, even if the subscription is designated for an individual.) Standing orders are accepted.

Single copies are available at $12.95 when payment accompanies order. (California, New Jersey, New York, and Washington, D.C., residents please include appropriate sales tax.) For billed orders, cost per copy is $12.95 plus postage and handling.

Substantial discounts are offered to organizations and individuals wishing to purchase bulk quantities of Jossey-Bass sourcebooks. Please inquire.

Please note that these prices are for the academic year 1987–88 and are subject to change without notice. Also, some titles may be out of print and therefore not available for sale.

To ensure correct and prompt delivery, all orders must give either the *name of an individual* or an *official purchase order number.* Please submit your order as follows:

Subscriptions: specify series and year subscription is to begin.
Single Copies: specify sourcebook code (such as, CD1) and first two words of title.

Mail orders for United States and Possessions, Australia, New Zealand, Canada, Latin America, and Japan to:
        Jossey-Bass Inc., Publishers
        433 California Street
        San Francisco, California 94104

Mail orders for all other parts of the world to:
        Jossey-Bass Limited
        28 Banner Street
        London EC1Y 8QE

New Directions for Child Development Series
William Damon, *Editor-in-Chief*

CD1   *Social Cognition,* William Damon
CD2   *Moral Development,* William Damon
CD3   *Early Symbolization,* Howard Gardner, Dennie Wolf

Contents

Editor's Notes

Over the past decade, we have seen an increasing interest in the health and well-being of adolescents. This interest has come during a decade when the national data on the health of adolescents suggest that adolescents are getting healthier. The measures that are currently used to formulate this "healthy" view of adolescents include mortality patterns, utilization of physician services, hospital discharge rates, and conditions cited in visits to office-based physicians (NCHS, 1984; Cypress, 1984). The national data used to formulate this optimistic view of adolescence place undue emphasis on proximal and biomedical outcomes rather than psychosocial affects or behaviors whose outcomes may be more distal. With this approach, new morbidities that may be prevalent in or associated primarily with adolescence may go unrecognized or unmeasured. Current data available on adolescents' lack of competency in reasoning and mathematical skills, low literacy, unemployment, eating disorders, school dropout rates, sexual activity, victimization rates, substance use, homicide, accidents, and suicide do not support the trend of a healthier adolescence (NCHS, 1984; Irwin, 1987).

A reconceptualization of health as optimal functional status may provide a better understanding of the broader issues affecting adolescents' health. Optimal functional status implies that defining a healthy adolescence necessitates a look at behaviors that act as antecedents to adult morbidities as well as the behaviors and conditions that are of immediate concern during adolescence. Childhood precursors of health problems manifested during adolescence would also be of concern within this life-span paradigm. The changing health status of children in the 1980s will affect the psychosocial resources and coping abilities of these children as they become adolescents (Rosenbaum and Starfield, 1986). With this expanding definition of health, there needs to be precision in the way in which the terms are designated in order to make clear what measures and outcomes will be indicative of health status. The current indicators of health status are disease focused, with mortality being one of the few outcomes measured, and are thus inadequate, given the proposed framework. Since the major causes of morbidity and mortality during adolescence are behaviorally generated (for example, sexual activity, substance use, recreational and motor vehicle use, and so on), there is a need to acknowledge and document components of social behavior that may have both positive and negative consequences (Irwin and Millstein, 1986). This sourcebook broadens the definition of health and provides critical information concerning adolescent social behavior for a better understanding of how psychosocial development is more intricately connected with health status.

1

A careful consideration of the psychosocial aspects of adolescent health does not negate the importance of the biological changes that occur during adolescence. For a careful review of the issues regarding the important interface of biological change and behavior, readers are referred to a special issue of the *Journal of Adolescent Health Care* (Orr, 1987) and the summary statement on hormonal aspects of behavior (Orr and Hodgeman, 1987).

The key concepts presented in these Editor's Notes are derived from the following four chapters and the extensive deliberations of a study group consisting of professionals from the disciplines of anthropology, pediatrics, psychology, and sociology, which convened at the National Invitational Conference on the Health Futures of Adolescents at Daytona Beach, Florida, in April 1986 (see Irwin and Vaughan, in press). Each author has carefully analyzed the issues raised by previous research and his or her own current research and proposed how these issues relate to health. The chapters do not provide definitive answers but raise crucial questions for consideration concerning an expanded view of health during adolescence.

The key concepts developed during the meeting were as follows:

1. Healthy adolescent development is fostered by providing a prolonged supportive environment during early adolescence, with graded steps toward autonomy.

2. Positive as well as negative developmental and healthy outcomes are associated with certain exploratory behaviors. A more precise conceptualization of "risk taking" is needed to study and distinguish between constructive exploration and potentially destructive behaviors occurring during adolescence.

3. The major biological and psychosocial changes occurring during adolescence are not necessarily associated with negative outcomes and instability. Adolescence is not inherently turbulent. Understanding positive growth, the acquisition of new skills and health-promoting behaviors, and the changing nature of interpersonal relationships deserve increased attention.

4. Healthy development is encouraged by a process of mutual, positive engagement between the adolescent and various adults and peers. This process should occur through family and other significant adults and take place in schools, health institutions, and the community.

5. Healthy development must be studied and viewed in relation to the various contexts within which it occurs. Demographic, socioeconomic, psychological, biological, sociological, and historical factors can modify the characterization of normal development.

Prolongation of a Supportive Environment for Adolescents

During adolescence, the challenge faced by the family is for increased adolescent autonomy. Early adolescents strive for increased psychological independence, requiring more flexible family boundaries and more egalitarian parent-child relations. With the emergence of formal operations, the adolescent is able to question parental norms and beliefs. As discussed by Baumrind in Chapter Four, a reorganization of rights, responsibilities, and personal relationships is necessary if the prolongation of a supportive environment is to serve the function of adolescent development. A popular shift in perspective concerning adolescent needs was initiated during the 1960s and reflected the belief that less supervision and earlier independence would better foster healthy development. Current research indicates, however, that early separation or emotional autonomy from family or significant adults can have a negative effect on the adolescent (see Steinberg and Silverberg, 1986; Steinberg, 1987). This negative effect can be manifested by an increased risk of alienation or susceptibility to negative peer influences and participation in "unhealthy" behaviors (such as substance use or premature sexual activity). Early distancing from parents or significant adults is more likely to have a negative impact in a number of situations. Important factors that appear to contribute to the early separation of adolescents from significant adults include early timing of pubertal development; authoritarian or permissive, as opposed to authoritative, parenting; family disruption and dysfunction; large and impersonal school environments; and immersion in a negative peer culture (Hamburg, 1974; Blyth, Simmons, and Carlton-Ford, 1983; Baumrind, 1971; Ogbu, 1981; Lewis and Lewis, 1984; Brooks-Gunn, Petersen, and Eichorn, 1985a; 1985b).

Empirical evidence for the benefits of a prolonged supportive environment is provided by studies demonstrating the negative effects of multiple, simultaneous transitions on self-esteem, academic performance, and problem school behavior. As discussed by Simmons in Chapter Two, adolescents seem to do better in terms of self-esteem and behavioral coping if there is some "arena of comfort" in their lives during periods of multiple changes. Additional evidence is provided by research on family attachments and susceptibility to negative peer pressure. Adolescent substance abuse, for example, may be less likely when social bonds and commitment to parents and prosocial others are strong regardless of parenting style. In some studies, authoritative parenting has been associated with increased competence in the adolescent, less susceptibility to antisocial influences, and a variety of other desirable outcomes. This parenting approach reflects open communication, give-and-take between parent and adolescent, and consistent support but also firm enforcement of unambiguous rules (Baumrind, 1971). In general, a supportive environment with adults who give guidance not only seems to act as a buffer against negative social influences but as a promoter of prosocial behaviors and skills as well. Authoritative parenting style is associated with desirable outcomes such as exploratory behavior and greater capacity for cooperative or responsible social relationships (Grotevant and Cooper, 1985).

Future national trends indicate that more adolescents of the late 1990s will come from impoverished, single-parent, and low-income minority families (see Rosenbaum and Starfield, 1986; Irwin, 1987). These situations increase the probability that individuals will enter adolescence with a more alienated view of the world. This alienation appears to place adolescents at greater risk for early separation and disengagement. With this projection, specific intervention programs that provide supportive "family" environments in nontraditional ways will need to be developed. Clinicians and researchers will need to ask the question: How can supportive environments be developed with the increasing number of nontraditional families?

A Precise Conceptualization of Risk-Taking Behavior

The linkage of numerous behaviors under one domain such as risk taking needs to be further validated empirically but is appealing for several reasons. This conceptualization provides a framework to (1) investigate groups of behaviors rather than a single behavior, (2) begin to address the positive and negative outcomes of certain behaviors, (3) understand whether certain behaviors are truly associated or are unrelated, and (4) understand the developmental trajectory of certain behaviors.

By using the term *risk-taking behavior,* issues begin to emerge concerning which behaviors one includes under this classification. Suicide, homicide, serious eating disorders, skydiving, sexual activity, reckless motor or recreational vehicle use, substance use and abuse, and mountain climbing have all been included under this construct. These behaviors are associated with a wide range of both negative and positive precursors and outcomes.

Inherent in the risk-taking terminology is an implication that the behavior is volitional, without a recognition of the contribution and influence of environmental forces or individual differences. With a careful analysis of the process of engaging in certain behaviors, some activities may be more reflective of risk avoidance than of risk taking. These situations would be more likely to arise when certain salient social pressures or other environmental factors encourage participation in certain risky behaviors. Research has demonstrated a positive correlation between susceptibility to peer pressure and negative risk taking (see Kandel, 1980, 1985). A young person may choose to avoid rejection by his or her peers, thus indicating less willingness for social risk taking.

There remains a need to distinguish between productive and destructive risk taking. Data from studies on peer learning and skill development in the sciences have shown greater skill acquisition in early adolescents who are more willing to try out ideas and who initially make more mistakes. Studies in this domain suggest that experimentation and taking chances within a controlled or positive context may be a desirable, adaptive, and normal aspect of healthy development (Damon, 1984). New terms may be necessary, such as *exploratory behavior*, for those acts associated with positive consequences. This conceptualization implies that negative behaviors traditionally labeled as risk taking can be distinguished from exploratory behavior or constructive risk taking by their undesirable effects on health and their tendency to impede positive psychosocial development. The process of risk taking, itself is thus not necessarily viewed as maladaptive. The personal and interpersonal resources one has available to cope with the risks, the antecedents associated with the behavior, and the nature of possible outcomes may determine whether behaviors are viewed as risky.

Additional definitional problems confound the area of risk taking. Many of the behaviors fall on a continuum and are not accurately represented by a dichotomous classification. Also, in certain situations, statistically normal behavior may be associated with negative health outcomes (for instance, substance use and abuse).

In the area of risk-taking research, there needs to be a greater emphasis on adolescents' own views of risk within the various social contexts in which they live. An abundant literature on adult risk perception exists, yet little is known about adolescents' perception of risk (Slovic, 1987; Koshland, 1987). What value is placed on possible outcomes such as rejection by peers or parents? Are behaviors labeled as negative by adults, such as persistent drug or alcohol use and promiscuous or premature sexual activity, perceived as such by the adolescent? Too often clinicians and researchers have made assumptions regarding the "invulnerable adolescent." Recent research is demonstrating that adolescents perceive many behaviors as dangerous and risky, but they nevertheless choose to engage in the behavior for the value placed on other perceived, anticipated, and experienced psychosocial outcomes of the behavior (Millstein and Irwin, 1985; Irwin and Millstein, 1987; Millstein and Irwin, 1987). Research is also needed to examine the mechanisms through which peers and adults can have a positive influence on risk taking and on the development of competency through socially sanctioned experimentation.

Increased Focus on Positive Aspects of Adolescence

Past research has been guided by the "storm and stress" perspective of adolescence and has focused on what goes wrong, went wrong, or is going wrong during adolescence. Less is known about what contributes to positive growth and health-enhancing behaviors.

As Hill and Gilligan point out in Chapters One and Three, research in the area of adolescence has been preoccupied with autonomy or separation, which primarily has been defined as freedom from parental influence. This overemphasis on autonomy has led to neglect in examining the development of other skills and orientations that are also valuable assets for productive living. Gilligan and Hill maintain that issues of attachment and the transformation of significant interpersonal relationships during adolescence have been largely overlooked. While substantial work has been done on empathy and sympathy as a moral/affective dimension, a care-focused orientation has not been thoroughly examined as a legitimate cognitive construct. Interdependence and the development of healthy interpersonal relationships are important aspects of adult functioning, and these skills, as well as the growth of independence, are not necessarily fostered in an environment where separation, minimal supervision, and autonomy are primarily valued. Hill maintains that a new conceptualization of autonomy is emerging and has been described as self-regulation as opposed to freedom from parents. Self-regulation appears to develop more effectively in families where attachment and commitment are valued.

Family styles in which the adolescent experiences both individuation and connectedness support identity exploration and rational competence. There is a need for research to focus on the determinants and outcomes of adolescents' close relationships with parents and additional significant others, including peers. In particular, there is a need to understand the quality and dimensions of relationships with these significant others, the functional roles they play (supportive versus challenging), and the nature and frequency of the activities they engage in with adolescents. The negative effects of relationships with peers are well documented. Little is known about the positive effects of peer interaction. Negative interactions in some contexts may have positive outcomes. Thus, while conflict among peers and families is generally viewed as a negative event, such conflict can produce an open sharing of views that prompts healthy decision making (Grotevant and Cooper, 1986; Powers and others, 1983). This type of conflict may provide the young person with a way to engage in exploratory behavior with a positive outcome. This approach has implications for health professionals who interact frequently with adolescents regarding health-promoting and damaging behaviors (such as compliance, diet, exercise). This behavior may enable adolescents to learn to articulate their concerns regarding health regimens.

Mutually Engaging Adolescents in a Positive Way

Over the past several decades, there has been an undue emphasis on independence and autonomy as the most crucial developmental outcomes of adolescence and on the development of the Piagetian cognitive processes. For most children, adolescence does not signal a total separation from family or dissolution of relationships with significant others. During the second decade, the interpersonal dynamics are merely transformed in response to the newly emerging abilities and social status of the adolescent. An emphasis on how relationships are maintained throughout the normal transitions of adolescence directs efforts toward finding mechanisms in which healthy engagement can occur. A constructive engagement process between adolescents and others must be bidirectional and reciprocal and acknowledge that even young adolescents are capable of reflective thinking and moral reasoning. Productive engagement requires that some legitimacy is given to the perspective of the adolescent, and communications about values or societal norms ideally are not authoritarian. Engagement ideally involves commitment and interacting within a value framework where rules are unambiguous. As Gilligan points out in Chapter Three, this process is hypothesized to foster health-promoting behavior by encouraging self-governance and personal commitment in regard to healthy lifestyles and by effectively transmitting those values that would discourage and be inconsistent with destructive behaviors (such as drug use, premature sexual activity, smoking, and so on).

Sources of engagement for adolescents should not be limited just to parents. In fact, there may be a multitude of ways and levels at which the engagement process can occur. The role of community factors and institutions such as schools, volunteer organizations, and government agencies in facilitating the engagement of youth in meaningful ways is in need of further study and planned-intervention research. The nature of the interpersonal engagement processes of adolescents with their significant others needs to be investigated in relation to value acquisition and, ultimately, behavior. The adolescent will not find a place in the community as a whole and may possibly develop a sense of alienation and isolation without a careful definition of the values of the society and the social conventions of the adult world. Opportunities to engage in the community can be structured to enable adolescents to broaden their knowledge and understanding of the varieties of vocations that are available to them; the education, training, and commitment they require from someone engaged in these vocations; and the satisfactions, demands, and disadvantages of the work. Structured job experiences and volunteer activities may also be useful to help adolescents realize that they have useful roles and can contribute productively to society (Greenberger, 1983). Many of the health-compromising behaviors of adolescents seem to reflect the lack of a meaningful role in the current world.

Adolescence in Multiple Contexts

Adolescence does not occur in isolation. The progression of adolescent development is partially determined by environmental and individual characteristics present prior to and during adolescence. Consequently, this life stage must be investigated and described with special attention to contextual factors. Serious misrepresentation of adolescence has occurred and will continue to occur if these multiple contexts are not clarified. In the four chapters that follow, all of the authors maintain the need to look at adolescence in its multiple contexts. Some of the more crucial characteristics that need to be included are demographics, socioeconomics, family structure, peer-group structures, work settings, historical (cohort) effects, and age of cohort (with reference to physiological and chronological ages).

To study adolescent development in reference to the specific contexts within which it occurs or among specific subgroups endorses the notion that theories and measures developed and tested for one group may not be appropriate for another. Recommending, for example, that healthy life-styles are only promoted by commitment and involvement by "intact" family members may fail to recognize the alternative sources of support and guidance that are available for those adolescents growing up in nontraditional yet statistically common settings. Defining and framing moral dilemmas from one perspective may preclude an understanding and development of effective intervention strategies for those having a different orientation. Significant misinterpretations of an adolescent's behavior or health status can also occur if no attempt is made to view his or her development with reference to parental life events and simultaneously occurring developmental changes. Parental and adolescent developmental status may interact within the family context.

These previous five concepts provide the framework for considering social behavior and health. The four authors of this volume were selected to represent a crucial perspective on an expanded view of adolescence and how it closely relates to health within the second decade of life.

In the first chapter, John Hill critically reviews what we know about families and adolescent development now and what we will need to know in the future in order to better understand the healthy development of young people and the families in which they live. Hill supports the notion raised later by Baumrind and Simmons that conflict in family relations is not the hallmark of adolescence or the need for adolescents to have an interdependent relationship with their families. Hill also elaborates on the concept of parental style as an essential component in the developmental process of adolescence. In raising this issue, he articulates the need to understand the role of social class and working patterns of parents, especially working mothers. In his review of autonomy, he clarifies the central nature of autonomy to the view of American society. With this background, he introduces the need for a new definition of autonomy as being self-governance. Hill points out that autonomy research has often dictated research on the family and that there is a need to investigate what contributes to the development of intimacy.

The second chapter by Roberta Simmons focuses on the social factors that make the adolescent's experience more or less difficult. In particular, Simmons carefully addresses the impact of school context and of school transition. In looking at school transition, Simmons is careful to raise questions about other factors (family structure, pubertal status, gender, type of school) that appear to intensify the reaction to school transition. She maintains that all transitions are not problematic. The reaction of the adolescent to the transition depends on the characteristics of the individual and the transition and the particular outcome at issue. Transitions that are marked by great discontinuity and that move an adolescent into an impersonal environment appear to be more difficult. Multiple simultaneous transitions and earlier transitions that do not provide an arena of comfort for the adolescent appear to create more problems for the adolescent.

In the third chapter, Carol Gilligan raises four reasons why adolescent development needs to be reconsidered. Her reconsideration stems from changes in the understanding of infancy and childhood, from the recognition that females have not been systematically studied, from a recognition that theories of cognitive development emphasize mathematical and scientific thinking with little or no attention to the humanities, and finally, from the fact that the psychology of adolescence is anchored in separation and independence rather than interdependence and commitment. Gilligan delineates the need to investigate development by shifting one's research methods to focus on the ways that people describe moral conflict they have confronted and discuss the choices they have made in their lives. From this new approach, a care-focused perspective has arisen. Gilligan also points out the need for professionals working with adolescents to take an authoritative stance, and yet she maintains that the individuals (mothers and teachers) who have the most contact with adolescents have little authority in our society. Beyond her own work, she urges researchers to integrate research that attempts to look at prosocial awareness and moral judgment.

In the fourth chapter, Diana Baumrind considers adolescent risk taking in contemporary America by first reviewing the crucial developmental issues that confront the adolescent and the role risk taking plays in the developmental process. Baumrind distinguishes between risk-taking behavior, which is characteristic of the adolescent stage of development and is adaptive, from those behaviors that are pathological expressions for which there is no secondary gain. Beyond her critique of the definitional issues, she raises important questions about the purpose of risk taking and how certain behaviors become destructive and may actually serve to alienate young people from our society, thereby providing no opportunity for exploratory or experimental processes which would be developmentally normal and serve as preparatory to commitment.

Conclusion

The issue of psychosocial development and adolescent health is not new; however, with the changing nature of the health problems of the second decade of life and with the major share of these problems being behaviorally generated, a careful and complete understanding of the nature of development provides a foundation for developing effective research programs that may foster the further initiation of intervention and prevention programs aimed at promoting the health and well-being of our future generations.

Acknowledgments

During the preparation of this introduction, the author was supported in part by the Division of Maternal and Child Health, Bureau of Health Care Delivery and Assistance, Department of Health and Human Services grant MCJ 000978; the William T. Grant Foundation; and the Robert Wood Johnson Foundation. The author would like to thank George Martin and Diane Wells for their assistance in the preparation of this manuscript. The material in this sourcebook was part of the work study group on Psychosocial Context of Adolescent Development, Research Issues, at the National Invitational Conference on the Health Futures of Adolescents, Daytona Beach, Fla., April 1986, which was sponsored by the Society for Adolescent Medicine and the Division of Maternal and Child Health. Support for the conference came from the Division of Maternal and Child Health, Bureau of Health Care Delivery and Assistance, Department of Health and Human Services. These Editor's Notes represent the efforts of several critiques by all members of the study group and the guidance, critique, and comments by Elaine Vaughan. I am deeply indebted to Elizabeth McAnarney for her vision during her presidency of the Society for Adolescent Medicine to encourage Don Orr and me to pursue the development of a conference on research issues in adolescent medicine. Don Orr diligently worked with me to develop the structure of the two study groups focusing on research at Daytona and he chaired the study group on hormonal aspects of normal and abnormal behavior. Final thanks go to Bob Blum who organized the overall conference.

Charles E. Irwin, Jr.
Editor

References

Baumrind, D. "Current Patterns of Parental Authority." *Developmental Psychology Monograph*, 1971, *4*, 1–103.

Blyth, D., Simmons, R., and Carlton-Ford, S. "The Adjustment of Early Adolescents to School Transitions." *Journal of Early Adolescence*, 1983, *3*, 105-120.

Brooks-Gunn, J., Petersen, A. C., and Eichorn, D. (eds.). "Timing of Maturation and Psychosocial Functioning in Adolescence, Part I." *Journal of Youth and Adolescence*, 1985a, *14* (3), entire issue.

Brooks-Gunn, J., Peterson, A. C., and Eichorn, D. (eds.). "Timing of Maturation and Psychosocial Functioning in Adolescence, Part II." *Journal of Youth and Adolescence*, 1985b, *14* (4), entire issue.

Cypress, B. "Health Care of Adolescents by Office-Based Physicians: National Ambulatory Medical Care Survey, 1980-81." National Center for Health Statistics publication no. 99. September 28, 1984, pp. 1-8.

Damon, W. "Peer Education: The Untapped Potential." *Journal of Applied Developmental Psychology*, 1984, *5*, 331-343.

Greenberger, E. "A Researcher in the Policy Arena: The Case of Child Labor." *American Psychologist*, 1983, *38*, 104-111.

Grotevant, H. D., and Cooper, C. R. "Patterns of Interaction in Family Relationships and the Development of Identity Exploration in Adolescence." *Child Development*, 1985, *56*, 415-428.

Grotevant, H. D., and Cooper, C. R. "Individuation in Family Relationships." *Human Development*, 1986, *29*, 82-100.

Hamburg, B. A. "Coping in Early Adolescence: The Special Challenges of the Junior High School Period." In S. Arieti (ed.), *American Handbook of Psychiatry*. Vol. 2. G. Caplan (ed.), *Child and Adolescent Psychiatry, Sociocultural and Community Psychiatry*. New York: Basic Books, 1974.

Irwin, C. E. "Building Bridges: Adolescent Health in the 1990s." Paper presented at the annual meeting of Maternal and Child Health Directors, Washington, D.C., April 1987.

Irwin, C. E., and Millstein, S. G. "Biopsychosocial Correlates of Risk-Taking Behaviors During Adolescence." *Journal of Adolescent Health Care*, 1986, *7*, 82S-96S.

Irwin, C. E., and Millstein, S. G. "The Meaning of Alcohol Use in Early Adolescence." *Pediatric Research*, 1987, *21* (4), 175A.

Irwin, C. E., and Vaughan, E. "Psychological Context of Adolescent Development: Research Issues." *Journal of Adolescent Health Care*, in press.

Kandel, D. B. "Drug and Drinking Behavior Among Youth." In J. Coleman, A. Inkeles, and N. Smelser (eds.), *Annual Review of Sociology*, New York: Hayworth, 1980.

Kandel, D. B. "On Processes of Peer Influences in Adolescent Drug Use: A Developmental Perspective." In J. Brook, D. Lettieri, and D. Brook (eds.), *Advances in Alcohol and Substance Abuse*. New York: Hayworth, 1985.

Koshland, D. (ed.). "Immortality and Risk Assessment." *Science*, 1987, *236*, 241.

Lewis, C., and Lewis, M. "Peer Pressure and Risk-Taking Behaviors in Children." *American Journal of Public Health*, 1984, *74*, 580-584.

Millstein, S. G., and Irwin, C. E. "Adolescent Assessment of Behavioral Risk: Sex Differences and Maturation Effects." *Pediatric Research*, 1985, *19* (4), 112A.

Millstein, S. G., and Irwin, C. E. "The Relationship Between Representations of Health and Illness." *Health Psychology*, 1987, *6* (6).

National Center for Health Statistics. *Health, United States, 1984*. Washington, D.C.: Government Printing Office, 1984.

Ogbu, J. U. "School Ethnography: A Multilevel Approach." *Anthropology and Education Quarterly*, 1981, *12*, 3-10.

Orr, D. (ed.). *Journal of Adolescent Health Care*, 1987, *8* (6), entire issue.

Orr, D., and Hodgeman, C. "Hormonal Aspects of Normal and Abnormal Behavior in Adolescents." *Journal of Adolescent Health Care*, 1987, *8* (6).

Powers, S. I., Hauser, S. T., Schwartz, J. M., and others. "Adolescent Ego Development and Family Interaction: A Structural-Developmental Perspective." In H. D. Grotevant and C. R. Cooper (eds.), *Adolescent Development in the Family*. New Directions for Child Development, no. 22. San Francisco: Jossey-Bass, 1983.

Rosenbaum, S., and Starfield, B. "Today's Children, Tomorrow's Youth." Paper presented at National Invitational Conference on Health Futures of Adolescents, Daytona Beach, Fla., 1986.

Slovic, P. "Perception of Risk." *Science*, 1987, *236*, 280–285.

Steinberg, L. "Single Parents, Stepparents, and the Susceptibility of Adolescents to Antisocial Peer Pressure." *Child Development*, 1987, *58*, 269–275.

Steinberg, L., and Silverberg, S. B. "The Vicissitudes of Autonomy in Early Adolescence." *Child Development*, 1986, *57*, 841–851.

"Utilization of Short-Stay Hospitals by Adolescents: United States, 1980." Public Health Service publication no. 93. September 14, 1983, pp. 1–5.

Further Sources

Baumrind, D. "Familial Antecedents of Adolescent Drug Use: A Developmental Perspective." In C. Jones and R. Battjes (eds.), *Etiology of Drug Abuse: Implications for Prevention*, Rockville, Md.: National Institute on Drug Abuse, 1985.

Brown, S. "The Health Needs of Adolescents in the United States." In *Healthy People: The Surgeon General's Report on Health Promotion and Disease Prevention*. Washington, D.C.: Government Printing Office, 1979.

Damon, W., and Hart, D. "The Development of Self-Understanding from Infancy Through Adolescence." *Child Development*, 1982, *53*, 841–864.

Eisenberg, N. *Altruistic Emotion, Cognition, and Behavior*. Hillsdale, N.J.: Erlbaum, 1986.

Gilligan, C. "New Maps of Development: New Visions of Maturity." *American Journal of Orthopsychiatry*, 1982, *52* (2), 199–212.

Greenberger, E., and Steinberg, L. *When Teenagers Work: The Psychological and Social Costs of Adolescent Employment*. New York: Basic Books, 1986.

Hill, J., and Holmbeck, G. "Attachment and Autonomy During Adolescence." In G. W. Whitehurst (ed.), *Annals of Development*. Greenwich, Conn.: Jai Press, 1986.

Irwin, C. E. "Why Adolescent Medicine?" *Journal of Adolescent Health Care*, 1986, *7* (6), 1S–12S.

Irwin, C. E., Shafer, M-A., and Millstein, S. G. "Pubertal Development in Adolescent Females: A Marker for Early Sexual Debut." *Pediatric Research*, 1985, *19* (4), 112A.

Charles E. Irwin, Jr., M.D., is associate professor of pediatrics and director of the Division of Adolescent Medicine at the University of California, San Francisco. His major research interest is in the biopsychosocial correlates of risk-taking behavior during adolescence.

Research on adolescents and their families has come of age over the past decade. Not only is there more research than ever before, but it is linked to the distinctive cognitive, social, and biological features of adolescence. The domain of investigation needs to be expanded to encompass ethnic families of color and issues of family structure.

Research on Adolescents and Their Families: Past and Prospect

John P. Hill

During the past decade, there have been remarkable changes in research on family-adolescent relations. There is more research: More investigators study adolescents than before, and research efforts are programmatic. For the first time, there is the promise of and the potential for the development of cumulative knowledge. Replications are underway in laboratories other than those in which the research was initiated, and cross-method "replications" are forthcoming. Pipelines now are full of work whose results promise to inform us over the next decade. There is a critical mass of investigators in place that has not existed before.

The quality of research on adolescents and families has increased as well. Conceptual and theoretical bases in the family process, family therapy, and developmental literatures often guide current inquiry. Current research is methodologically more "mainstream" as well. Attention to psychometric issues has increased. Attention to the reliability of observations in laboratory and field settings is more sophisticated than before. Results of sequential analyses soon will be emerging in print. Methodological hegemonies are giving way to productive blends of survey/questionnaire/interview, standardized instrument, observational, laboratory, but not yet experimental, approaches.

C. E. Irwin, Jr. (ed.). *Adolescent Social Behavior and Health.*
New Directions for Child Development, no. 37. San Francisco: Jossey-Bass, Fall 1987.

The most implicative developments for the future are that parent-adolescent research no longer is dominated by notions initially developed to understand early experience or by knee-jerk acceptance or rejection of *Sturm und Drang* views. Simple and sovereign notions about identification, internalization, and imitation, or about conflict and rebelliousness have been discredited. It cannot be taken for granted, media messages aside, that the second decade of life is any more characterized by "transitional" or "conflictual" issues than any other period or transition in the life course. The research currently in process is oriented, in unprecedented degree, to the distinctive features of adolescence—to biological and cognitive change—and to adolescent's roles in transforming family interactions, family relationships, and enduring intraindividual characteristics.

Unfortunately, the kinds of families that are being studied bear little relation to the kinds of families in which most adolescents now grow up in America. There is no existing body of archival quality research on adolescence in Afro-American, Asian-American, Hispanic-American, or Native-American family contexts. Similarly, there is little research on families conceived in other than "Dick and Jane" terms. (The "Dick and Jane" family is composed of a working father, a housewife mother, and two or more children.) Research on divorce and its effects on younger children has increased over the past decade, but there is little work that focuses on adolescents. We know little about adolescent rearing in single-parent and reconstituted families. The striking gap in our knowledge is the domain of ethnic and structural variations in adolescent family life.

What follows is perhaps overshadowed by this conclusion. Deservedly so. I shall return to these matters of ethnicity and family composition in the final section of this chapter, which is organized around the following themes: conflict, authoritative parenting, and autonomy.

Conflict

While clinicians and the media continue to stress the normality of conflict and rebelliousness in family relations during the adolescent era, available data offer no support for such views. For the past twenty years, responsible reviewers have concluded that contentious interchange and systemic disorganization are not characteristic of family relations during adolescence (see Bandura, 1964; Hill, 1980; Montemayor, 1983). Survey studies are consistent in reports of conflict in 15 percent to 25 percent of families. Most such studies are cross-sectional. The few longitudinal studies available suggest the same conclusion. Offer and Offer (1975) found that 21 percent of high school males experienced "tumultuous growth," including conflictful parent-child interactions.

Few studies have been designed to permit comparisons of the incidence of conflict before and during adolescence. One noteworthy exception is the longitudinal work on development on the Isle of Wight. Rutter and others (1976) found that confrontations between parents and adolescents occurred once a month for 11 percent of the boys and 7 percent of the girls. Nearly 25 percent of the parents of boys and 9 percent of the girls reported some emotional withdrawal or communication difficulty. The majority of these parents reported that communication difficulties or emotional withdrawal had always been presented. Rutter and others (1976) found that already disordered families were three times more likely than normal families to experience alienated relationships during adolescence. Overall, as Montemayor (1983) concludes, there is no evidence for an increase in conflict from childhood to adolescence.

When conflicts do occur, mundane issues predominate: Family chores, hours, dating, grades, personal appearance, and eating habits are the matters of concern. These issues have not changed much over the decades. In one of the first studies of this sort, Lynd and Lynd (1929) found in their study of Middletown that hours and home duties were most often subject to disagreement, and club and society membership and religious observance were least often subject to disagreement. In a 1982 replication of this study, Caplow and others (1982) found that the issues viewed by adolescents as most and least likely to lead to conflict with parents were the same as had been reported in 1929. Despite rapid social change and extensive media attention to generational differences, especially during the late 1960s and early 1970s, study after study has confirmed that parent-adolescent conflicts about basic economic, religious, social, and political values are rare.

Available data on positive aspects of parent-adolescent relations are complementary to those on conflict. The majority of adolescents report feelings of closeness and positive regard for parents (Bandura, 1964; Douvan and Adelson, 1966; Kandel and Lesser, 1972). Despite increases in leisure time spent with peers and decreases in time spent in family activities, positive cognitive and affective orientations toward parents appear to characterize the adolescent era. Further corroboration comes from studies in which adolescents are asked to anticipate possible consequences of parental and peer disapproval. The majority of adolescents believe that parental disapproval would be more difficult to accept than breaking with a friend (Bowerman and Kinch, 1959; Coleman, 1961; Csikszentmihalyi and Larson, 1984; Rutter and others, 1976). Epperson's (1964) data in fact suggest that teenagers are more concerned than younger children about parental disapproval.

Finally, parents continue to exercise considerable influence upon basic values during the second decade of life. Adolescents agree with their parents on most basic value issues and report value sharing more often than value conflict (Bengston, 1970; Douvan and Adelson, 1966; Jennings and Niemi, 1975; Kandel and Lesser, 1972; Offer, 1969). Especially noteworthy here is the continued influence of parents on adolescents' achievement aspirations (Spenner and Featherman, 1978). Best friends do come to have substantial influence on educational and vocational aspirations during the second decade of life, but parents continue to account for most of the variance in adolescents' ambitions. Rutter's (1980, p. 31) assessment is apt.

> The overall conclusion must be that although young people's leisure activities with their peers increase during adolescence and although their shared activities with parents decrease, nevertheless in the great majority of cases, parent-adolescent relationships remain generally harmonious, communication between the generations continues and young people tend both to share their parent's values on the major issues of life and also to turn to them for guidance on most major concerns. The concept of parent-child alienation as a usual feature of adolescence is a myth.

Authoritative Parenting

Factor analyses of parenting behavior (whether during childhood or adolescence) typically yield two primary dimensions: warmth-hostility (sometimes labeled acceptance-rejection) and autonomy-control (Martin, 1975). Studies of these dimensions are ubiquitous in the literature on adolescent rearing. Virtually all behavioral outcomes likely to be valued by practitioners and middle-class parents are at least modestly correlated with parental warmth, especially self-esteem (Maccoby and Martin, 1983). Baumrind (1968) has taken these dimensions (and other correlated dimensions) into account in proposing a trichotomous classification of parenting behavior. She argues that *authoritative* parenting produces instrumentally competent children. Authoritative parents are supportive but not smothering, make their standards known, value disciplined behavior monitored by self-control, and provide reasons and explanations for their standards and actions (and expect their children to do the same). *Authoritarian* parents are less likely to reason with or explain to their children. They offer orders rather than engaging in discussions. They are obedience centered and dogmatic. *Permissive* parents respond in a benignant way to the child; they are resources that the child may or may not use. Either affectionate or emotionally uninvolved, permissive parents are not very active socializing agents. For some of these parents, granting freedom serves to avoid child-rearing responsibilities.

Research shows considerable evidence for the importance of the behaviors reflected in these clusters and for their utility in interpreting parental behavior (for examples, see Bandura and Walters, 1959; Douvan and Adelson, 1966; Kandel and Lesser, 1972). Aspects of authoritative parenting are widely implicated in behavioral outcomes that are usually considered "normal" or "healthy" during adolescence (Hill, 1980).

We do not yet have a comprehensive understanding of why authoritative parenting "works" for adolescents. Given existing literature based largely on studies of younger children, we may speculate that authoritative parenting is effective because authoritative parents more often model the kinds of psychosocial outcomes studied. Their greater acceptance of the child may promote greater emulation. They are more nurturant, and their approval may have greater reward value. Withdrawal of that approval may also be a more potent sanction. Because they may be less frustrating, authoritative parents may less often induce emotional responses that could interfere with the use of the more complex social-reasoning processes of which adolescents are capable. It is probable that the effects of authoritative parenting are multiply determined.

Two important conclusions follow: For practitioners, the concept of authoritative parenting is important, owing to its conjoint emphasis on parental acceptance and warmth; parental assertiveness around rules, norms, and values; and—especially during adolescence—of parents' capacities to listen, explain, and openly negotiate (even if, or especially because, in the final round, the parents' standards will prevail). For researchers, given the correlational nature and yet the coherence of the existing literature, the task is to increase understanding of the processes involved.

Baumrind (1968) has suggested that explanation is particularly central to effective adolescent rearing. The absence of parental explanation often is implicated in undesirable outcomes (such as alienation from parents and lack of initiative, responsibility, and self-confidence) because peremptory demands actually delegitimate parental authority. Emerging cognitive capabilities make it possible for the adolescent to read social situations in as complex a way as parents can. By not offering explanations, parents fail to acknowledge the fundamental changes that have occurred. At present we lack the longitudinal data that it would take to test and expand our understanding of Baumrind's formulation, but it seems likely that authoritarian parents may well be less responsive to intraindividual change in their children at early adolescence than are authoritative parents.

Studies of social class differences in parenting behavior have shown that more authoritarian strategies are employed in families lower in the stratification systems (Hess, 1970). In a now classic set of studies, Kohn (1977) has shown that fathers involved in work tasks that are simple and repetitive, that require working with one's hands and with things more than with other people and ideas, and that are very closely supervised are more likely to value conformity to authority (obedience) than self-control in their children. Kohn's important contribution has been to explain social class effects by reference to parents' conditions of work.

Parenting practices in the middle-class tend to emphasize the child's intent. In working-class families, the consequences of the child's actions are emphasized. The middle-class child is punished on the basis of intent, and the lower-class child, on the basis of the consequences of transgression. Kohn's work (which has focused largely on families with prepubescents) is germane to understanding adolescence because virtually every attribute held to be a positive outcome of adolescence by developmentalists depends on the development of self-direction (autonomy, intimacy, principled moral reasoning, identity, ego development) rather than obedience.

Kohn's formulation is not without difficulties, chief among them the role of the mother in the process. As Turner (1980, p. 971) pointed out, it is puzzling "how the adult male's occupational role can decisively shape the child's socialization when we all know that most of our children are socialized chiefly by their mothers, whose worlds are quite different." Turner's observation invites the question, among others, of how paternal work-related values may be mediated by maternal behavior. And there is the fact that most mothers now work as well. In general we need to know far more than we do now about how conditions of maternal as well as paternal work—and not just the fact of work—impact on family life during the adolescent era.

Autonomy

Striving for independence is likely to rank high on old-fashioned lists of typical adolescent needs or tasks. Doubtless this prominence is largely owing to the centrality of the independence theme in American culture. According to the Handlins (1971, p. 78) in their history of American youth and American families, facing life meant leaving home, the latter was "an inescapable circumstance of the approach to maturity in an unstable and expanding society." Freedom as both a political philosophy and as a style of life has, from the days of the frontier society, been linked with impending maturity.

Paradoxically, however, the invention of adolescence has been associated with preventing young people from growing up too fast. For both Rousseau ([1762] 1911) and Hall (1904), and for those reformers who supported child labor laws, compulsory education, and juvenile justice laws, modern city life was the enemy, leading to dreaded precocity. Delaying the transition to adulthood was held to be the greater good not only for society but for the individual.

This theory aside, what do we know about the development of autonomy during the second decade of life? Surprisingly little, if what is meant is the rebelliousness that many associate with a normal adolescence. Rebelliousness is a label likely to be invoked by adults to explain any teenage behavior that is disliked. In fact, there has not been a single serious empirical study of rebelliousness yet reported in the literature. Those invested in rebelliousness must make do with operational definitions of autonomy that are less dramatic. Most common among these are self-reports of subjective autonomy (Elder, 1963; Kandel and Lesser, 1972), self-reports of participation in family decisions affecting the adolescent (Douvan and Adelson, 1966; Kandel and Lesser, 1972), confidence in personal decision making (Elder, 1963), and choices between parent-endorsed and peer-endorsed alternatives (Berndt, 1978; Brittain, 1963; Larson, 1972). (In the latter instance, choices favoring peers are assumed to provide information about independence.) What we know from this research is that however either is measured, authoritarian rearing is associated with low autonomy and authoritative rearing with high autonomy. The cross-cultural study by Kandel and Lesser (1972) is the best of this research, and their findings serve to illustrate the literature in general.

Kandel and Lesser examined the peer and family relations of American and Danish secondary school students. Their operational definition of autonomy was the extent to which the respondents felt that "both parents give me enough freedom." While Danish adolescents were more inclined to experience subjective autonomy than were American adolescents, relations among autonomy and other variables were the same in both countries. The feeling of having been granted independence was associated with avowed closeness and positive feelings, participation in family activities, seeking out parents for advice and support, and wanting to be like one's parents as an adult. The number of young people who talked over their problems with their parents increased over the high school years from 19 percent to 48 percent. Those adolescents with subjective feelings of independence less frequently saw their parents as old-fashioned and less frequently reported either more difficulty in getting along with them than in the past or conflict in their relations with them.

Authoritarian decision making in families in both countries decreased over the high school years, the number of specific rules for adolescents decreased, and the frequency of explanations increased. At the same time, subjective feelings of independence increased but never to the same level in the United States as in Denmark. Autonomy, at least as it is indexed by subjective feelings of freedom, is not associated with giving up a positive emotional relationship with parents, or with rebelliousness, or with turning away from parents as sources of social influence, or associated with high degrees of family conflict. Freedom during adolescence is associated with continuing, positive relationships with parents.

The coherence of the research available on autonomy is astonishing, given its theoretical, conceptual, and methodological crudity (see Hill and Holmbeck, 1986; Hill and Steinberg, 1976). The research reported so far, for example, is not noted for its attention to the concept of autonomy. Implicit in the common operations employed to measure autonomy is a conceptual definition that focuses on independence, essentially freedom from parental influence. This approach ignores the fact that most adult children maintain close relationships with their parents and continue to be influenced by them as well as by additional significant others in their lives. Definitions of autonomy that leave the adolescent free or independent are misleading and incomplete in that they fail to account for the continuing influence of significant others during and after adolescence.

One direction future research might take is based on another definitional focus, self-governance. This focus permits asking questions about the kinds of familial contexts and socialization practices that foster the development of self-regulatory processes. Matters then become not those of some vaguely defined freedom but of the regulation and modulation of impulses, of initiative and responsibility, and the like.

Two contemporary programs of research address such matters, those of Grotevant and Cooper (1982a, 1982b, 1985) and of Hauser and his colleagues (1984). Grotevant and Cooper have attempted to define dimensions of family interaction that bear on identity exploration (if not autonomy, certainly related to it). Their approach has been characterized by close attention to the family process, family development, and family therapy literatures as well as by the careful development of concepts of family interaction (individuation, permeability) that are coordinate with the developmental outcome of interest. They found, for example, that the "formulation of a distinctive sense of self appeared related to the adolescent's ability to express both openness to the views of others and differentness from others in the family" (1982a).

Hauser and others (1984) have focused on family interaction and ego development (again, an outcome variable focused, in part, on self-regulatory processes). On the family interaction side, enabling and constraining interactions are coded according to a theoretical scheme influenced by Stierlin (1974). On the ego development side, the work has been influenced by the conceptual and methodological efforts of Loevinger (1976). Their findings indicate that adolescent ego development is positively related to many of the enabling behaviors (explaining, acceptance, empathy) and negatively related to many of the constraining behaviors (judging, distracting, and devaluing). Sequential analyses are in process. Overall, both the Grotevant and Cooper work and the Hauser work suggest that family interaction variables are related to indices of adolescent autonomy. Many of these variables involve the appreciation of others as distinct (separateness, permeability, explanations), while others suggest supportiveness (empathy, acceptance, mutuality).

Also worthy of note is the consistency between these findings (based on the observation of family interaction) and earlier findings (based on questionnaires). The important role of explanation identified some years ago in questionnaire studies is echoed in the newer observational work, with its emphasis on negotiation. Thus, according to Grotevant and Cooper (1985, p. 20), autonomy (when considered in light of self-regulatory outcomes) seems to be "gained in the context of progressive and mutual redefinition of the parent-child relationship rather than by the child simply leaving the relationship."

In addition to its conceptual weaknesses, most of the traditional work on autonomy has been theoretically uninformed as well. Reviews of this work have frequently examined its relevance to psychoanalytic theory (as I have above in relation to the issue of conflict), but there is very little work that has been designed with the testing of this (or any other) theory in mind.

The autonomy focus at the core of psychoanalytic theory is labeled *detachment* from parents (Blos, 1979; Freud, [1958] 1969). The pubescent must deal again with both active and passive preoedipal and oedipal ties to his or her parents. Investments in nonincestuous, genital-sexual relationships with peers are held to require decathexis (that is, detachment) from infantile representations of parents. Maturity requires the de-idealization of parental images. The view of parents as omniscient, omnipotent, and omninurturant needs to be relinquished. The social-cognitive aspects of psychoanalysts' views have come to be more appreciated over the past decade. Smollar and Youniss (1985) report changes in children's perceptions of parents (especially mothers) consonant with psychoanalytic notions; there is direct de-idealization. Parents come to be perceived as less than perfect and less than all knowing. There is increasing recognition of mothers' (but less often of fathers') human and personal sides. Steinberg and Silverberg (1985) have reported similar results in a preliminary report of a longitudinal study of autonomy, which includes a de-idealization component. In general, de-idealization is held to be important for autonomy because it lays the groundwork for establishing oneself as a separate person with perspectives that can be different from those of the parents. White and others (1985) have begun to report findings from their longitudinal study of individuation and attachment in groups of twenty-two-, twenty-four-, and twenty-six-year-olds. One focus of their program of research is on relationship maturity. Affective, behavioral, and cognitive aspects of maturity in the parent-adult child relationship are measured through their Family Relationships Interview. Three levels of relationship maturity are described. In Level 1 (self-focused), the individual's view of the other is cognitively simple, often cast in terms of goodness and badness and rightness and wrongness. Affect is described as reactive, simple, and undifferentiated (love or hate, pleasure or aversion). Typical behavioral tendencies reported are generalized inclinations to approach or avoid the other. According to White and others (1985, p. 10),

Whether highly dependent or counterdependent, self-focused individuals appear to be too lacking in their own self-development or individuation to be able to bring anything much in the way of differentiated, articulated, and self-reflective functioning to their close relationships with others.

Level 2 (role-focused) individuals' relationships are dominated by conformity and conventionality. Close relationships are invested in because they are perceived as normative. Others are not seen as individuals, and concerns with roles and norms predominate. Affect is somewhat more differentiated than at the self-focused level but still is "stereotyped, bland, and controlled." While behavioral tendencies are somewhat more differentiated than the "either/or" of the self-focused, they tend to be responsive to stereotyped cognitions and expectations of what is "appropriate." At Level 3 (individuated-connected), individuals are both highly individuated themselves and also able to connect with close others in intimate, reciprocal, mutual bonds (White and others, 1985, p. 11). Differences are valued as contributing to relationships. Views of others and of self are well differentiated and well integrated. There is an appreciation of the complexity of the functioning of self and others. Preliminary results suggest that few subjects can, in fact, be placed at the individuated-connected level. Maturity scores with mothers are higher than scores with fathers. Typically, females' relationships are at higher levels than those of males. De-idealization and other transformations in representations of parents apparently extend well into the third decade of life.

The emerging influence of cognitive-developmental theories on parent-adolescent research should not go unremarked. While many theorists such as Selman, Kohlberg, and Loevinger have postulated the emergence or consolidation of distinctive phases of representation and reasoning during adolescence—some even labeled *autonomy*—these formulations are just now beginning to find their way into family research in relation to both the self-governance and the detachment foci of autonomy and other family socialization issues. (In addition to cognitively oriented efforts already cited, see Collins, 1985; Dix, 1985; Smetana, 1985.) Further studies of interrelations among intraindividual cognitive change, family interaction, and family relationships are forthcoming and should be encouraged, especially since cognitive change is one of the distinctive features of adolescence itself.

Another such distinctive feature is biological, namely the pubertal cycle. In a longitudinal follow-up of Steinberg and Hill's (1978) earlier cross-sectional study, Steinberg (1981) found that change in adolescent sons' pubertal status was significantly related to changes in family behaviors on a structured family interaction task (SFIT). At the apex of puberty, mothers interrupted their sons more than they did either earlier or later in the pubertal cycle. With advancing pubertal development, sons interrupted their mothers more, deferred to them less, and both sons and mothers explained themselves less. Mothers also deferred more to their sons after pubertal apex. With increasing maturity, sons interrupted their fathers less and deferred to them more, and fathers interrupted their sons more and deferred to them less. Sons gained influence in family decisions, at the expense of the mother.

Results for mother-son interaction confirmed the findings of the earlier cross-sectional study with very few exceptions. It appears that temporary perturbations occur in mother-son relations at or near the peak of pubertal growth. Results for father-son interaction were different. The cross-sectional data had suggested patterns similar to those for mothers and sons. The longitudinal data showed, instead, increasing dominance by the father and complementary submissiveness by the son. The results conform to accounts of dominance behavior in the primate literature: As the male begins to approximate adult status, he is increasingly deferred to by females and himself defers to larger males of higher status (see Steinberg, 1981).

In our study (Hill and others, 1985b), we have sought to "replicate" Steinberg's findings with a more modest, cross-sectional, and questionnaire approach. Similar findings emerged. For the mother-son dyad, relations between observer's ratings of pubertal status and several rearing and child outcomes variables were characteristically quadratic. Family Rules and Standards (child report) and Child Oppositionalism (mother report) were at their highest levels, and Family Activities (mother report) and Parental Satisfaction (mother report) were at their lowest levels in the apex pubertal group. On the other hand, less conflict was reported in the father-son dyad, a finding consistent with the dominance-submissiveness results obtained by Steinberg (1981).

For girls the findings to date are somewhat different than those that emerged for boys. In order to aid us in interpreting our observational findings for girls, we initially examined relations between menarcheal status and the rearing and child outcomes as reported on questionnaires (Hill and others, 1985a). Rather than quadratic trends, cubic trends were characteristic of the data. (Menarche was rated by parents and their seventh-grade daughters as: "has not yet begun," "has begun within the last six months," "has begun within the past twelve months," or "has begun longer than twelve months ago.") Perturbations in Family Rules and Standards (child report), Parental Acceptance (child report of mother), Family Activities (mother report), and Parental Influence (child report of mother) seem to occur six months after menarche, but by twelve months after, the mean values look much like those of the premenarcheal group. (Negative linear trends were also found for some of the father variables.) When we examined those families where daughters experienced menarche more than twelve months ago, the variable means look much like those of the six-months-ago group. For those girls whose menarche occurs relatively on time (within the past year), the relations look much like the quadratic relations reported by Hill and others (1985), Steinberg (1981), and Steinberg and Hill (1978) for boys. When menarche occurs early, however, it appears that the perturbations are not temporary but may instead persist.

The observational findings support and extend these questionnaire findings. Cantara (1983) found very similar cubic trends in his study of family interaction patterns around menarche in early adolescent girls. In the six-months-ago and the more-than-twelve-months-ago groups, mothers were rated as less affiliative, and they interrupted other family members more frequently. Fathers' interactions were rated as more affiliative. Mothers behaved in passive-aggressive ways toward fathers. Unlike boys, girls did not gain in influence at the expense of either the mother or father. Although perturbations in parent-daughter relations appear to characterize the period just after menarche, shifts in the dominance-submission patterns do not seem to occur in families with daughters in the same way and/or to the extent that they occur in families with sons. Sequential analyses are planned to elucidate further the role of conflict in adaptation to pubertal change (see Hill and Holmbeck, 1985).

The focus on autonomy in this chapter accurately reflects the attention it has received in the research relationship to other psychosocial issues. It is important that we continue to improve our understanding of changes in family behavior, interaction, relationships, and systems in relation to the development of self-governance. It would be misleading, however, to conclude that there are not other equally important intraindividual characteristics that are influenced by family relations. We have very little understanding, for example, of what changes in family relations during adolescence contribute to the development of intimacy. Capacities for relatedness, connectedness, communion, and for what Gilligan (this volume) has termed a "caring morality" have, given our preoccupation with freedom, been little studied. Cooper, Grotevant, and Ayers-Lopez's (1986) work on the interface between family interaction and negotiation with peers provides a model for subsequent efforts of this sort. Cross-contextual studies have a special claim to our attention during adolescence, especially if it is the case, as some have speculated, that modulation of aggressive impulses, learning of intimacy skills, experimenting with sexuality, and autonomous moral reasoning can occur seriously only in the peer group (see Hartup, 1977; Piaget, 1932). Studies in which familial and peer influences are considered within the same design are vital to our increased understanding.

The focus on adolescent autonomy is misleading too because it draws attention to the adolescent alone as the object of developmental focus. Parents are developing persons, and many are likely to be dealing with developmental issues complementary to those of their children: physical attractiveness and bodily integrity and vocational aspirations and realities. It is unlikely that we will fully understand adolescent development in the context of the family without a more articulate focus on parents as developing persons and the complementarity of their issues and those of their children.

Ethnic and Structural Variations in Adolescent Family Life

Within the past thirty years, major changes have taken place in the composition of families in America. According to Hodgkinson (1985, p. 3), "In 1955, 60% of the households in the U.S. consisted of a working father, a housewife mother, and two or more school age children. In 1980, that family unit was only 11% of our homes, and in 1985 it is 7%, an astonishing change."

Dick and Jane families are far from being modal. This startling fact calls for a sweeping change in consciousness in relation to the term family. And obviously, research based on samples of Dick and Jane families is coming to have and will continue to have lesser utility as a base for practice or even further research. (Although, insofar as it is the mother who continues to have the major child-rearing responsibility and most existing research is focused on mother-child dyads, our existing empirical and conceptual base is not totally without value.)

There is a pressing need for studies of several kinds.

1. Studies of maternal role satisfaction and the impact on adolescents and families are badly needed. Existing studies of effects on younger children suggest that overall role satisfaction is more crucial to familial and child outcomes than is the fact of work outside the home itself (Hoffman, 1984; Montemayor and Clayton, 1983). The old working versus nonworking paradigm is not likely to yield much useful information.

2. Studies of paternal role satisfaction are also needed. The available literature has implicated paternal job loss and job frustration in child and adolescent abuse (Hoffman, 1984). We know little outside of clinical observation about this phenomenon. There is no systematic literature on effects of paternal job satisfaction on spousal and parenting roles and their concomitant impacts on children or adolescents. Models taking direct effects and indirect effects (through the spousal relationship) on adolescents into account need to be developed. Job and role dissatisfaction may be particularly important if it occurs as the family is attempting to cope with other crises or developmental changes. Some of our own data suggest, for example, that coping with menarche is more difficult for fathers with high job dissatisfaction than those with low dissatisfaction and more difficult for mothers with high job satisfaction than those with low job satisfaction.

3. Hodgkinson (1985, p. 3) notes, "Of every 100 children born

today, 40 will be born to parents who divorce before the child is 18 and 5 will be born to parents who separate before the child is 18." Studies of effects of divorce on adolescents need to be pursued. (The bulk of the existing literature focuses on younger children.) Recent work from the Block, Block, and Gjerde (forthcoming) longitudinal study suggests the importance of prospective studies in this area, given that the constellation of factors supposed to be a result of divorce is already present prior to divorce. Studies focusing on early adolescence are especially important, given that adaptations to biological change may be impacted. Similarly, newly present or emerging cognitive capabilities may modify or moderate the experience of divorce.

4. Studies of single-parent families are essential. Again, according to Hodgkinson (1985, p. 3), "The Census tells us that 59% of the children born in 1983 will live with only one parent before reaching age 18—this now becomes the NORMAL childhood experience." Especially needed are studies designed with due attention to the primary phenomena of adolescence.

5. Studies of reconstituted families should have a high priority. Existing research on family dissolution and reconstitution focuses almost entirely on families of younger children, yet as Hetherington and Camara (1984, p. 422) comment, "Adolescents, particularly those in the custody of the remarried parent, appear to have the most complex reactions." Nine- to fifteen-year-olds are less likely to accept even a good stepparent than are younger or older children. Recent work by Anderson, Hetherington, and Clingempeel (1986) suggests that the kinds of transformations in family interactions reported by Steinberg (1981) and Hill and others (1985a, 1985b) do not emerge in reconstituted families. Studies of families where adolescents are involved in the reconstitution are needed, as are studies of youngsters who become adolescent within the context of an already blended family.

6. Changes in family forms create new family needs that require community attention. It seems likely that services and programs are continuing to be designed and operated for Dick and Jane families, yet we have little understanding of the community resources (formal and informal) needed or used by single-parent or reconstituted families that include adolescents. According to Bronfenbrenner, Moen, and Garbarino (1984, p. 321), "It is a reflection of the present state of knowledge (or, perhaps better said, state of ignorance) that we have not been able to find a single study that compared the community experience of children of different ages or of families at different stages of the life cycle." What kinds of community characteristics are associated with family behaviors, interactions, relationships, and systems that enhance healthy or unhealthy outcomes in adolescence? We have barely begun to find out.

In concluding their review of research on family dissolution and reconstitution, Hetherington and Camara (1984, pp. 430–431) offer the following assessment:

> It is clear that there are differences in the way children of different ages and adults at different points in the life cycle respond to divorce, yet little is known about the psychological or social factors that mediate these differences. In addition, to date, there are no methodologically sound studies of the processes of family dissolution or remarriage among black, Hispanic, or other ethnic groups. Nor are there systematic studies of the phenomena of family changes among lower-income families. As we have noted in our review, there is tremendous variation in children's and parents' responses to divorce and remarriage. Given the diversity of cultural and ethnic backgrounds of those experiencing dissolution and remarriage, it is reasonable to expect that the experience of divorce for Caucasian middle-income families cannot be generalized to all other ethnic and socioeconomic groups.

Ethnic groups of color—Afro-Americans, Asian-Americans, Hispanic-Americans, Native-Americans—made up 20 percent of the U.S. population in 1983. It is predicted that (owing especially to the greater relative increase of Hispanic-Americans) persons of color may outnumber Anglo-Americans in the U.S. population by the end of the century. Understanding adolescence in America now and in the future presupposes a far greater investment in research on ethnic families of color than is now being made (or even seriously anticipated). What should this research look like?

In their recent review of the literature on ethnic families of color, Harrison, Serafica, and McAdoo (1984) conclude that rigorous studies of ethnic families are limited not only in number but also by relative inattention to (1) changing roles of family members and how these changes affect relationships within the family and the functions served by the contemporary ethnic family, (2) the social values and socialization goals of different ethnic groups, (3) impacts of specific child-rearing practices on particular developmental outcomes, and (4) linkages to contemporary theories about families and development. Existing research, minimal as it is, has been conceptualized in nonethnic and middle-class terms or in light of a "social problems" approach wherein emphases on deficit, disadvantage, and deprivation circumvent inquiry into the dynamics of ethnic family life. Harrison, Serafica, and McAdoo's assessments should be helpful in guiding future parent-adolescent research. Such research would benefit, too, from attention (within the same designs) to (1) adaptation to intraindividual change, (2) conditions and consequences of parental employment,

28

(3) community contexts and resources, (4) the developmental issues of parents, and (5) concurrent peer relations.

References

Anderson, E. R., Hetherington, E. M., and Clingempeel, W. G. "Pubertal Status and Its Influence on the Adaptation to Remarriage." Paper presented at the Biennial Meetings of the Society for Research on Adolescence, Madison, Wisc., April 1986.

Bandura, A. "The Stormy Decade: Fact or Fiction?" *Psychology in the Schools,* 1964, *1,* 224-231.

Bandura, A., and Walters, L. H. *Adolescent Aggression.* New York: Ronald Press, 1959.

Baumrind, D. "Authoritarian vs. Authoritative Control." *Adolescence,* 1968, *3,* 255-272.

Bengston, V. L. "The Generation Gap: A Review and Typology of Social-Psychological Perspectives." *Youth and Society,* 1970, *2,* 7-32.

Berndt, T. J. "Developmental Changes in Conformity to Peers and Parents." *Developmental Psychology,* 1978, *15,* 608-616.

Block, J. H., Block, J., and Gjerde, P. F. "The Personality of Children Prior to Divorce: A Prospective Study." Forthcoming.

Blos, P. *The Adolescent Passage.* New York: International Universities Press, 1979.

Bowerman, C. E., and Kinch, J. W. "Changes in Family and Peer Orientation of Children Between the Fourth and Tenth Grade." *Social Forces,* 1959, *37,* 206-211.

Brittain, C. V. "Adolescent Choices and Parent-Peer Cross-Pressures." *American Sociological Review,* 1963, *28,* 385-291.

Bronfenbrenner, U., Moen, P., and Garbarino, J. "Child, Family, and Community." In R. D. Parke (ed.), *Review of Child Development Research.* Vol. 7. *The Family.* Chicago: University of Chicago Press, 1984.

Cantara, A. R. "Pubertal Status and Assertiveness in Family Interaction in Early Adolescent Girls." Unpublished master's thesis, Virginia Commonwealth University, Richmond, 1983.

Caplow, T., Bahr, H. M., Chadwick, B. A., Hill, R., and Williamson, M. H. *Middletown Families.* Minneapolis: University of Minnesota Press, 1982.

Coleman, J. S. *The Adolescent Society.* New York: Free Press, 1961.

Collins, W. A. "Cognition, Affect, and Development in Parent-Child Relationships: The Transition to Adolescence." Paper presented at the Biennial Meetings of the Society for Research in Child Development, Toronto, April 1985.

Cooper, C. R., Grotevant, H. D., and Ayers-Lopez, S. "The Interface Between Adolescents' Interactions with Families and Peers: Three Models." Paper presented at the Biennial Meetings of the Society for Research on Adolescence, Madison, Wisc., April 1986.

Csikszentmihalyi, M., and Larson, R. *Being Adolescent.* New York: Basic Books, 1984.

Dix, T. "Parental Inferences About Children in Developmental Change." Paper presented at the Biennial Meetings of the Society for Research in Child Development, Toronto, April 1985.

Douvan, E., and Adelson, J. *The Adolescent Experience.* New York: Wiley, 1966.

Elder, G. H. "Parental Power Legitimation and Its Effect on the Adolescent." *Sociometry,* 1963, *25,* 50-65.

Epperson, D. C. "A Reassessment of Indices of Parental Influence in 'The Adolescent Society.'" *American Sociological Review,* 1964, *29,* 93-96.

Freud, A. "Adolescence." In *The Writings of Anna Freud: Research at the Hampstead Child-Therapy Clinic and Other Papers* (1956-1965). Vol. 5. New York: International Universities Press, 1969. (Originally published 1958.)

Grotevant, H. D., and Cooper, C. R. *Identity Formation and Role-Taking Skill in Adolescence: An Investigation of Family Structure and Family Process Antecedents.* Bethesda, Md.: National Institute of Child Health and Human Development, 1982a.

Grotevant, H. D., and Cooper, C. R. "Individuation in Family Relationships." *Human Development,* 1982b, *29,* 82-100.

Grotevant, H. D., and Cooper, C. R., "Patterns of Interaction in Family Relationships and the Development of Identity Exploration in Adolescence." *Child Development,* 1985, *56,* 415-428.

Hall, G. S. *Adolescence: Its Psychology and Its Relations to Physiology, Anthropology, Sociology, Sex, Crime, Religion, and Education.* New York: Appleton, 1904.

Handlin, O. H., and Handlin, M. F. *Facing Life: Youth and the Family in American History.* Boston, Mass.: Little, Brown, 1971.

Harrison, A., Serafica, F., and McAdoo, H. "Ethnic Families of Color." In R. D. Parke (ed.), *Review of Child Development Research.* Vol. 7. *The Family.* Chicago: University of Chicago Press, 1984.

Hartup, W. W. "Adolescent Peer Relations: A Look to the Future." In J. P. Hill and F. J. Monks (eds.), *Adolescence and Youth in Prospect.* Guilford, England: IPC Science and Technology Press, 1977.

Hauser, S. T., Powers, S. I., Noam, G. G., Jacobson, A. M., Weiss, B., and Follansbee, D. J. "Familial Contexts of Adolescent Ego Development." *Child Development,* 1984, *55,* 195-213.

Hess, R. D. "Social Class and Ethnic Influence on Socialization." In P. H. Mussen (ed.), *Carmichael's Manual of Child Psychology.* New York: Wiley, 1970.

Hetherington, E. M., and Camara, K. A. "Families in Transition: The Processes of Dissolution and Reconstitution." In R. D. Parke (ed.), *Review of Child Development Research.* Vol. 7. *The Family.* Chicago: University of Chicago Press, 1984.

Hetherington, E. M., Cox, M., and Cox, R. "Divorce and Remarriage." Paper presented at the meetings of the Society for Research in Child Development, Boston, Mass., April 1981.

Hill, J. P. "The Family." In M. Johnson (ed.), *Toward Adolescence: The Middle School Years. The Seventy-Ninth Yearbook of the National Society for the Study of Education.* Chicago: University of Chicago Press, 1980.

Hill, J. P., and Holmbeck, G. N. "Familial Adaptation to Pubertal Change: The Role of Conflict." In W. A. Collins (chair), *Parent-Child Relations in the Transition to Adolescence: Family Adaptations to Pubertal Change.* Symposium conducted at the meeting of the Society for Research in Child Development, Toronto, April 1985.

Hill, J. P., and Holmbeck, G. N. "Attachment and Autonomy During Adolescence." In G. W. Whitehurst (ed.), *Annals of Child Development.* Vol. 3. Greenwich, Conn.: JAI Press, 1986.

Hill, J. P., Holmbeck, G. N., Marlow, L., Green, T. M., and Lynch, M. E. "Menarcheal Status and Parent-Child Relations in Families of Seventh-Grade Girls." *Journal of Youth and Adolescence,* 1985a, *14,* 301-316.

Hill, J. P., Holmbeck, G. N., Marlow, L., Green, T. M., and Lynch, M. E. "Pubertal Status and Parent-Child Relations in Families of Seventh-Grade Boys." *Journal of Early Adolescence,* 1985b, *5,* 31-44.

Hill, J. P., and Steinberg, L. D. "The Development of Autonomy During Adolescence." Paper presented at the Symposium on Research on Youth Problems Today, Fundacion Faustino Orbegoza Eizaguirre, Madrid, Spain, 1976.

30

Hodgkinson, H. L. *All One System: Demographics of Education, Kindergarten Through Graduate School.* Washington, D.C.: Institute for Educational Leadership, 1985.

Hoffman, L. W. "Work, Family, and the Socialization of the Child." In R. D. Parke (ed.), *Review of Child Development Research.* Vol. 7. *The Family.* Chicago: University of Chicago Press, 1984.

Jennings, M., and Niemi, R. "Continuity and Change in Political Orientations: A Longitudinal Study of Two Generations." *American Political Science Review,* 1975, *69,* 1316-1375.

Kandel, D. B., and Lesser, G. S. *Youth in Two Worlds: United States and Denmark.* San Francisco: Jossey-Bass, 1972.

Kohn, M. L. *Class and Conformity.* (2nd ed.) Chicago: University of Chicago Press, 1977.

Larson, L. E. "Influences of Parents and Peers During Adolescence: The Situation Hypothesis Revisted." *Journal of Marriage and the Family,* 1972, *34,* 67-74.

Loevinger, J. *Ego Development: Conceptions and Theories.* San Francisco: Jossey-Bass, 1976.

Lynd, R. S., and Lynd, H. M. *Middletown.* New York: Harcourt Brace Jovanovich, 1929.

McAdoo, H. P. "Demographic Trends for People of Color." *Social Work,* 1982, *27,* 15-23.

Maccoby, E. E., and Martin, J. A. "Socialization in the Context of the Family: Parent-Child Interaction." In P. H. Mussen (ed.), *Handbook of Child Psychology.* Vol. 4. New York: Wiley, 1983.

Martin, B. "Parent-Child Relations." In F. D. Horowitz (ed.), *Review of Child Development Research.* Vol. 4. Chicago: University of Chicago Press, 1975.

Montemayor, R. "Parents and Adolescents in Conflict: All Families Some of the Time and Some Families Most of the Time." *Journal of Early Adolescence,* 1983, *3,* 83-103.

Montemayor, R., and Clayton, M. D. "Maternal Employment and Adolescent Development." *Theory into Practice,* 1983, *56,* 415-428.

Offer, D. *The Psychological World of the Teenager.* New York: Basic Books, 1969.

Offer, D., and Offer, J. B. *From Teenage to Young Manhood: A Psychological Study.* New York: Basic Books, 1975.

Piaget, J. *The Moral Judgment of the Child.* New York: Free Press, 1932.

Rousseau, J. *Emile.* (B. Foxley, trans.) London: Dent, 1911. (Originally published 1762.)

Rutter, M. *Changing Youth in a Changing Society: Patterns of Adolescent Development and Disorder.* Cambridge, Mass.: Harvard University Press, 1980.

Rutter, M., Graham, P., Chadwick, O., and Yule, W. "Adolescent Turmoil: Fact or Fiction?" *Journal of Child Psychology and Psychiatry,* 1976, *17,* 35-56.

Smetana, J. G. "Family Rules, Conventions, and Adolescent-Parent Conflict." Paper presented at the Biennial Meetings of the Society for Research in Child Development, Toronto, April 1985.

Smollar, J., and Youniss, J. "Transformations in Adolescents' Perceptions of Parents." Paper presented at the Biennial Meetings of the Society for Research in Child Development, Toronto, April 1985.

Spenner, K., and Featherman, D. "Achievement Ambitions." *Annual Review of Sociology.* Vol. 4. Palo Alto, Calif.: Annual Reviews, 1978.

Steinberg, L. D. "Transformations in Family Relations at Puberty." *Developmental Psychology,* 1981, *17,* 833-840.

Steinberg, L. D., and Hill, J. P. "Patterns of Family Interaction as a Function of

Age, the Onset of Puberty, and Formal Thinking." *Developmental Psychology,* 1978, *14,* 683–684.

Steinberg, L. D., and Silverberg, S. B. "The Vicissitudes of Autonomy in Early Adolescence." Paper presented at the Biennial Meetings of the Society for Research in Child Development, Toronto, April 1985.

Stierlin, H. *Separating, Parents and Adolescents.* New York: Quadrangle, 1974.

Turner, R. H. "Review of *Class and Conformity: A Study in Values* by M. L. Kohn." *American Journal of Sociology,* 1980, *85,* 969–971.

White, K. M., Speisman, J. C., Costos, D., and Smith, A. "Relationship Maturity: A Conceptual and Empirical Approach." Paper presented at the Third Biennial Conference on Adolescent Research, Tucson, Ariz., March 1985.

Further Sources

Atkinson, B. R., and Bell, N. J. "Attachment and Autonomy in Adolescence." Paper presented at the biennial meeting of the Society for Research on Adolescence, Madison, Wisc., April 1986.

Becker, W. C. "Consequences of Different Kinds of Parental Discipline." In M. L. Hoffman and L. W. Hoffman (eds.), *Review of Child Development Research.* Vol. 1. New York: Russell Sage, 1964.

Blos, P. *On Adolescence: A Psychoanalytic Interpretation.* New York: Free Press, 1962.

Braungart, R. C. "Youth and Social Movements." In S. E. Dragastin and G. H. Elder (eds.), *Adolescence in the Life Cycle: Psychological Change and Social Context.* London: Halsted, 1975.

Gilligan, C. F. "Adolescent Development Reconsidered." Paper presented at the National Conference on Health Futures of Adolescents, Daytona Beach, Fla., 1986.

Gustafson, B. *Life Values of High School Youth in Sweden.* Stockholm: Institute of Sociology of Religion, 1972.

Hill, J. P., and Monks, F. J. "Some Perspectives on Adolescence in Modern Societies." In J. P. Hill and F. J. Monks (eds.), *Adolescence and Youth in Prospect.* Atlantic Highlands, N.J.: Humanities Press, 1977.

Schaefer, E. S. "A Circumflex Model for Maternal Behavior." *Journal of Abnormal and Social Psychology,* 1955, *59,* 226–235.

Stolte-Heiskanen, V. "Social Indicators for Analysis of Family Needs Related to the Life Cycle." *Journal of Marriage and the Family,* 1974, *36,* 592–600.

John P. Hill, Ph.D., is professor of psychology at Virginia Commonwealth University. His major research interest is in social relations during adolescence with particular attention to effects of puberty on psychosocial adaptation.

*When investigating the impact of social transition on deprived
and nondeprived adolescents, one should consider the
abruptness of the change, other simultaneous transitions,
and the availability of at least one unchanging arena of
comfort. More research is needed on the short- and long-term
effects of impersonality in the social context and on the effects
of the proximate environment.*

Social Transition and Adolescent Development

Roberta G. Simmons

In terms of mental health and social behavior, entry to adolescence is difficult for some but not for other youngsters. The social factors that make the adolescent's experience more or less difficult are worthy of consideration. This chapter focuses on what is known about the effect of one major social context on the child: the impact of school context and of school transition. I shall also consider the effects of other factors that intensify the reaction to school transition. First, however, I shall review the arguments concerning the overall difficulty of entry to adolescence as a life period.

Adolescence as a Difficult Period

Substantial controversy has been generated within the behavioral sciences concerning the difficulty of adolescence as a transitional period.

This work has been funded by NIMH grant R01 MH-30739 and a grant from the William T. Grant Foundation. In addition, the work of the author has been supported by a Research Development Award from the National Institute of Mental Health, number 2 K02 MH-41688. The author wants to especially thank Professor Candace Kruttschnitt for her help.

C. E. Irwin, Jr. (ed.). *Adolescent Social Behavior and Health.*
New Directions for Child Development, no. 37. San Francisco: Jossey-Bass, Fall 1987.

Some characterize the period as an exceptionally stressful time in the life course. Hall (1904) originally described the adolescent years as ones of "storm and stress." Later, Erikson (1959, 1968) characterized adolescence as a time of identity crisis, and psychoanalysts such as Blos (1962, 1971) and Anna Freud (1958) theorized that puberty sparks a resurgence of oedipal conflicts for the boy and preoedipal pressures for the girl (see Barglow and Schaefer, 1979). According to Elkind (1967, 1984), cognitive processes and premature pressures toward adulthood also contribute to adolescent difficulty. From the sociological and anthropological point of view, adolescence in the United States has been described as a period of physical maturity and social immaturity and as a time of discontinuity and of status ambiguities. Excellent reviews of this approach to adolescence as stressful can be found in Offer and Offer (1975), Offer, Ostrove, and Howard (1981) and Weiner (1970).

More recently, to many investigators the supposed tumult of adolescence is just that—supposed and mythical (see Petersen and Taylor, 1980). They have concluded that for most youngsters, these years are not marked by stress or turmoil (see Grinker, Grinker, and Timberlake, 1962; Offer, 1969; Weiner, 1970; Bandura, 1972; Coleman, 1974; Moriarty and Toussieng, 1975; Haan, 1977; Savin-Williams and Demo, 1984). In some cases, the investigators compare levels of one or more variables across ages and fail to find the adolescents scoring more negatively than younger children (Attenborough and Zdep, 1973; Bowman, 1974; see Wylie's review, 1979). Alternatively, stability coefficients and/or factor structures are compared over the years, and no break is seen at the entry into adolescence. (Monge, 1973; Dusek and Flaherty, 1981; see also Engel, 1959; and Carlson, 1965). It is probably safe to conclude that while some children find adolescence difficult, a high proportion, perhaps the majority, do not. Even where there is difficulty, these problems do not necessarily generalize across psychological or behavioral attributes or assume severe proportions.

The extent of difficulty experienced on transition to adolescence depends on the outcome area at issue, the characteristics of the particular transition, and the characteristics of the individual. In fact, examination of different outcome areas leads to different conclusions about adolescent difficulty. This point is exemplified when three key outcome areas in adolescence are compared: self-esteem, school grades, and deviant behavior. First, in terms of self-image, Wylie (1979) concludes that there is no patterned, consistent relationship of age to self-concept and, across studies, no pattern of increasingly negative self-image in adolescence. In fact, recent reviews of large-scale longitudinal studies report a consistent rise, not a drop, in self-esteem as children move from early to late adolescence (see Kaplan, 1975; McCarthy and Hoge, 1982; O'Malley and Bachman, 1983). There is more controversy concerning the fate of self-esteem and other aspects of self-concept during the transition between childhood and early adolescence. While some studies show no age difference (Attenborough and Zdep, 1973; Coleman, 1974), others indicate worsening near, or on entry to, adolescence, that is, in Grades 6, 7, or 8 or ages 12 through 13 compared to earlier ages (Piers and Harris, 1964; Katz and Zigler, 1967; Yamamoto, Thomas, and Karns, 1969; Jorgensen and Howell, 1969; Trowbridge, 1972; and Soares and Soares, 1970). (For mixed results, see Bohan, 1973; Monge, 1973; Protinsky and Farrier, 1980; Metcalfe, 1981; Dusek and Flaherty, 1981; Harter, 1982).

It is possible that much of the inconsistency across studies can be linked to variability in their methodology. The longitudinal studies showing a rise in self-esteem during adolescence are based on large, representative samples and probably can be trusted (O'Malley and Bachman, 1983). However, many of the studies comparing children to early adolescents are not as compelling, although they identify an important potential problem. All are cross-sectional, some have small samples (Piers and Harris, 1964; Katz and Zigler, 1967; Bohan, 1973). Only a few indicate they used random sampling (Katz and Zigler, 1967—a suburban sample; Yamamoto, Thomas, and Karns, 1969—a suburban sample; Attenborough and Zdep, 1973—a national household sample).

Interestingly, even though there have been fewer large-scale random-sample studies of the entry into adolescence than of movement through adolescence, several authors suggest that the early adolescent years may well be the most crucial time of adolescence with respect to stressors and distress (Grinker, Grinker, and Timberlake, 1962; Hamburg, 1974; Offer and Offer, 1975; Douvan and Adelson, 1966; Steinberg and Hill, 1978). Major current large-scale studies in the United States are those of Simmons and Blyth (1987), Petersen (1983), Duke and others (1982), and Eccles (1984).

Whatever the course of self-esteem during adolescence, grade point average appears to decline with age, particularly as students change into junior high and then into senior high schools (Simmons and Blyth, 1987; Felner, Ginter, and Primavera, 1982). Rather than reflect difficulty with school work, this trend may be due to more difficult grading standards by teachers of older students. However, even so, a negative change in school success presents the child with a potential source of stress.

One clear area where there is unfavorable change in adolescence involves deviant behavior. Higher rates of deviant behavior in adolescence than in childhood or adulthood fit with a picture of difficult adjustment in the teenage years (particularly among males). However, it should be noted that different societies define deviant behavior differently; some would even classify as normal behaviors what we consider criminal (Black, 1983). Even in our own society there is an expectation that adolescents will experiment, and some deviant behavior and violation of rules is expected rather than clearly condemned. Erikson's (1968) concept of "psychosocial moratorium" is relevant here. In fact, a sizable proportion of adolescents do experiment, with only a smaller group committing acts highly problematic to society and indicative of difficulty in adjustment (Blumstein, Farrington, and Moitra, 1985).

There is an enormous literature on juvenile delinquency, which cannot be covered here. (For excellent reviews see Johnson, 1979; Kandel, 1980; Rutter and Giller, 1984; Elliott, Huizinga, and Ageton, 1985). The important point, however, is that such deviant behavior has significant implications for adolescent adjustment as well as for the well-being of these individuals when they become young adults (Jessor, 1983).

It is unlikely that the increase in deviant behavior in adolescence is a simple reflection of increased strength and independence. For most individuals, deviant behavior declines in adulthood when individuals are still physically strong and independent although testosterone levels may have decreased (Gove, 1985). Current focus on the reasons for decline after adolescence as well as on the reasons for the increase during adolescence may yield a pay-off in terms of policy suggestions for prevention of delinquency (Blumstein, Farrington, and Moitra, 1985). Of course, one contribution to the high adolescent delinquency rate in the past was the fact that one whole class of behavior, so-called status offenses, was considered deviant only when enacted by nonadults. Most states have now separated juvenile status offenses from their former delinquency classification. In any case, such status offenses cannot account for the generally high incidence of deviance among youth.

To understand adolescent difficulty, it is important to specify not only the outcome area at issue but also the characteristics of the particular transition. The school transition is an important one to consider.

School as a Context

The average youth spends at least seven hours of each weekday in school; approximately 40 percent of his or her working weekday hours. Thus, there is every reason to expect the nature of this environmental or ecological context to be important to the individual's adjustment (Bronfenbrenner, 1970).

Particularly relevant are the scheduled changes in schools that occur at entry to adolescence. As the individual moves out of childhood into and through adolescence, he or she makes a transition out of small, intimate elementary school contexts into larger and more impersonal schools. The question arises whether such a change is difficult for the youngsters.

The change is from a primary type context to a secondary context. The distinction between primary and secondary groups has received major attention in classical sociological theory (Toennies, [1887] 1940). This contrast has been emphasized by many of sociology's most important theorists including, among others, Durkheim, Cooley, and Parsons. It has a meaning above and beyond the usual definition in education of primary (early) and secondary (advanced) schools. It involves a contrast between intimate, intense, and total (diffuse) relationships, on the one hand, and impersonal, superficial, discrete, and specific relationships, on the other. The nuclear family is one of the key examples of the primary group; the large-scale bureaucracy is a frequent example of a secondary group.

Thus the movement from a more primary to a more secondary context is one of the many important changes that occur in adolescence. At some time in life, individuals who live in modern urban centers have to learn to cope with the large, impersonal, departmentalized, secondary-type organizations so characteristic of the larger society. The question is whether this transition can occur too early or in too stressful a manner for larger numbers of adolescents. The fact that there are many different types of transitions commonly made at entry to adolescence in the United States allows investigation of some of these issues. Many children at grade 7 switch into large junior high schools; others remain in intimate kindergarten through eighth grade (K–8) schools; still others transfer earlier into middle school systems.

In fact, the exact point at which youngsters first move into large organizational environments has changed drastically in the United States over the last fifty years and also differs radically from society to society (Blyth and Karnes, 1981). In the United States from 1900 to 1970, there was a dramatic decrease in the number of traditional four-year high schools and a marked increase in the number of junior high schools. In the past two decades, there has been a new movement into the middle school system in which the switch to a new school often precedes adolescence, that is, it occurs in grade 5 or 6.

These school transitions vary in the level of impersonality to which the child is subjected. Some schools are small, with the children remaining with the same teacher and schoolmates throughout the day. Some are large and departmentalized, with teachers and classmates changing several times throughout the day. One could hypothesize that impersonality would be difficult for the child. An impersonal school should be particularly difficult in a large city, where more of the students in a school are likely to be strangers than in smaller, more rural, or suburban contexts.

School transitions vary in the degree of discontinuity between old and new schools. A discontinuous change is one that is sudden and abrupt rather than gradual and one that involves great difference between the pre- and posttransition periods. In a classic article, Benedict (1954) characterizes adolescence in general in American society as an example of a maximally discontinuous status transition. The concern here is not with societal differences but with differences within our society between school transitions. The Benedict hypothesis could lead one to predict that youth who experience more discontinuity in environmental contexts will react more negatively (see Elder, 1968; Glaser and Strauss, 1971; Ogbu, 1982).

The Junior High School. Most studies of adolescents fail to report type of school structure and the timing of school transitions. Comparatively few school studies are longitudinal, and most research on transition is based on nonurban, nonrandom, or small samples.

Several experts have identified the large junior high school as difficult for the child (Hamburg, 1974; Lipsitz, 1977). The work of the author has indicated negative effects of the transition into the junior high at entry to adolescence (Simmons, Rosenberg, and Rosenberg, 1973; Blyth, Simmons, and Carlton-Ford, 1983; Simmons and Blyth, 1987). There is evidence that transition into a large impersonal school at ages 12 through 13 may be too early for many youngsters. In the author's work, such students are compared to grade 7 peers in a K-8 school who are not required to make any switch into a large, new school until they are two years older. When this comparison is made in grade 7, the junior high students turn out to be at a disadvantage in several important ways that were not evident the year before the transition. In junior high, key attitudes toward school become more negative than in the K-8 schools: Self-esteem and leadership show a decline for girls; participation in extracurricular activities, GPAs, and math achievement scores are less high and/or change less favorably for both genders; and levels of victimization (being robbed, threatened, or beaten) are higher for boys.

Furthermore, in two key respects, youngsters, especially girls, do not recover in middle adolescence from these early losses. They do not recover in terms of their self-esteem and their extracurricular participation and leadership. In grades 9 and 10, the girls who attended junior high are still showing less favorable scores than their K-8 counterparts. The K-8 students appear to have gained an advantage from remaining in an intimate school until an older age. The K-8 students switch for the first time into a new, large school in grade 9 (ages 14 through 15) rather than in grade 7 (ages 12 through 13).

These results have been viewed as compatible with a developmental readiness hypothesis, a hypothesis that individuals can be thrust too early into the next period in the life course; in this case they can be thrust too early out of childhood into adolescence. These results do not support an alternate stress inoculation hypothesis. The stress inoculation hypothesis posits that, for most children, experiencing one environmental change will better prepare them for the next similar transition than will protection from the early change. The children who have experienced the move into a large junior high school do not demonstrate a more favorable reaction to the senior high transition than do the K-8 youth who have never made such a prior school change. In fact, on average, in terms of self-esteem and participation in activities, the junior high cohort (especially girls) indicate more, not less, negative reaction after the entry to senior high school.

The more intense and longer-term reaction of girls to the junior high transition may be due to effects on their friendshp networks. In Karweit and Hansell's words (1983, p. 129): "The transition to junior high school may be particularly difficult for young females, precisely because of the interruption in strong interpersonal ties at which they are adept."

There is some evidence, outside of the author's work, of negative effects of the junior high compared to the elementary school. (See the large-scale study by Eccles, Midgley, and Adler, 1984; Reuman, 1984; and studies by Katz and Zigler, 1967.) However, comparisons of K–8 to junior high schools do not always favor the K–8 school. (See McCaig, 1967, and Wood, 1973, for two studies based in the suburbs.)

The Middle School. Whatever advantages to the K–8 system, there are relatively few K–8 schools in the United States at the moment, and it is unlikely that the clock will turn backward to create them. Rather, middle schools are becoming more prevalent (Blyth, Hill, and Smyth, 1981; Lipsitz, 1977). Many middle schools extend from grades 5 through 7 or grades 6 through 8 and thus involve an earlier, first transition. One could predict that middle schools, which involve an earlier transition, would be easier for children, especially if these schools are smaller in size than the usual junior high school. There is an opportunity for the middle school transition to be perceived as more gradual and less discontinuous than the junior high transition, especially if the transition brings with it a less dramatic increase in numbers of peers and in numbers of older children in the school.

Aside from size, the earlier transition might have the advantage of coinciding less with other adolescent changes: There would be less cumulative change. Although the definition of boundaries of adolescence are ambiguous in our society, entry to a new school in grade 5 or 6 (ages 10 or 11) is likely to be perceived as predating adolescence. Thus, the change is less likely to be treated symbolically as a movement into a very new age period and is less likely to trigger a new set of expectations by parents and teachers. Therefore, the child will less likely be pressured to adopt adolescent behaviors and relinquish childhood patterns. In addition, for most youngsters, especially boys, this change will precede much of pubertal development. Most boys will not have entered their height growth spurt and most girls will not have begun to menstruate, although other aspects of pubertal development will have begun. Thus, children could accustom themselves to a change in schools before having to cope with pubertal changes and changes in others' expectations of them.

In fact, the literature that compares junior high schools and middle schools sometimes favors the middle school (Mooney, 1970; Rankin, 1969; Schoo, 1970) but not always (Harris, 1968; Reid, 1983; Wood, 1973). Once again, for the most part, these are not studies with large random samples in urban contexts. The study of Blyth, Hill, and Smyth (1981) in a large city with a representative sample supports the hypothesis that seventh-

and eighth-grade students will find the entry to adolescence easier in a middle school that excludes ninth graders.

Whatever the year of transition, it should be noted that there is likely to be a top-dog, bottom-dog effect. The author's research shows that many social-psychological advantages accrued when the children were the oldest students in the school, and many disadvantages accrued when they were the youngest (Simmons and Blyth, 1987).

It could also be hypothesized that whenever the early adolescent child is the youngest in the school, he or she is more likely to be victimized and that older children are more likely to be the perpetrators, at least while they retain an advantage in physical strength. However, the study by Boesel and others (1978), based on a large survey of youth, questions whether older children are the prime victimizers, even in junior high school when they are the strongest.

School Characteristics. In addition to exploring the effects of school grade structures, it is also relevant to ask which particular school characteristics ease the transition into adolescence. It should be noted that investigators with a different focus have questioned the importance of between-school characteristics. Influenced by Coleman and others (1966), several studies in the last decade concluded that between-school differences, especially with respect to school resources, had little effect on educational achievement. What did have an impact were the background characteristics children brought to the school (see Alwin and Otto, 1977; Hauser, Sewell and Alwin, 1976; Bachman, O'Malley, and Johnston, 1978; Bachman and O'Malley, 1980; Johnston, 1973).

Critics of this conclusion raise several arguments. First, criticisms have been leveled relative to statistical analysis. It has been claimed that joint effects of home and school have been attributed only to home (selection) factors (Anderson, 1982; Bidwell and Kasarda, 1980), that multiplicative and interactive effects involving schools are not being investigated, and that longitudinal studies are needed. (Sørenson and Hallinan, 1977; Alexander, McPartland, and Cook, 1981). In-depth studies of unusual schools (outliers and schools with excellent reputations) appear to show consistent differences between these and more average schools (Lipsitz, 1984; Lightfoot, 1983). In addition, investigators have argued that the importance of school factors should not be dismissed despite their small effects, since such factors can be altered, unlike many of the background variables that have larger effects (Summers and Wolfe, 1977; Rowan, Bossert, and Dwyer, 1983; Purkey and Smith, 1983). Also, many of the early studies focused on differences among high schools, while it is possible that school differences matter more for younger children and early adolescents (Entwisle and Hayduk, 1982; Alexander, McPartland, and Cook, 1981).

Finally, critics claim that the right school characteristics were not being examined in studies that showed no effect. While major structural characteristics and resources had little consequence, effects were produced by status composition, by microstructural or more proximate characteristics (such as tracking, departmentalization, ability grouping, degree and type of teacher control, reward structure, level of student participation, classroom characteristics, stability of student body), and by climate or school culture.

In regard to the transition into adolescence, the issue of adequate physical and emotional protection of the child could be raised. Lipsitz (1984) and Lightfoot (1983) emphasize the importance of physical safety as a school characteristic, and the author's results indicate that children who have been victimized (robbed, threatened, beaten) in school by other children develop lower self-esteem (Simmons and Blyth, 1987). Lipsitz (1984) reports also that middle schools known for their excellence are more likely to demonstrate a structure more like that of an elementary rather than a more bureaucratic senior high school. In this light, one set of key school characteristics appears to have received less than its due of attention. Most studies have not focused on characteristics that should increase or decrease feelings of impersonality, anonymity, and discomfort in the school. Size of school, of course, is such a factor. Elkind (1984) hypothesizes that large schools should intensify adolescent distress; Berkovitz (1979) posits contradictory effects of size on children. On the one hand, large school size may foster alienation, isolation, and difficulties with communication and intimacy. On the other hand, there are many new opportunities, including the opportunity to meet a variety of peers from various backgrounds.

Barker and Gump (1962) and Simmons and Blyth (1987) note that proportionately fewer students participate in extracurricular activities in a large school (although there are more activities), and Brookover and others (1979) show mixed effects on academic self-concept. A good number of studies, however, show no significant effects of school size on achievement or aspirations (McDill and Rigsby, 1973; Flanagan and others, 1962; Ramsøy, 1961) or on a wider range of dependent variables (Rutter and others, 1979).

More relevant than the size of the total school may be the size and continuity of the child's more proximate groupings in the school. Hawkins and Berndt's (1985) research suggests that the negative effects of a large junior high school can be mitigated by smaller, stable, intimate subgroup environments within the school. Other factors that may increase anonymity but which are little studied include departmentalization, lack of stability in peer groups throughout the day, multiple teachers, busing schedules that limit extracurricular participation, and school feeder patterns that fail to keep together large cohorts of children who know each other from one school to the next. Rutter and others (1979) do show lower delinquency levels among students in England who remain with the same group of peers since starting in a school.

Similarly, Lipsitz (1984, p. 182) describes some excellent middle schools that divide students into small subgroupings and extend the time that subsets of students remain together during the day and over a period of several years, and she concludes: "Antisocial behavior that results from the randomness and brevity of student groupings in most secondary schools is substantially reduced in these schools."

The extracurricular structure in a school can also affect feelings of community versus anonymity as well as the rank structure among students (Morgan and Alwin, 1980, Epstein and Karweit, 1983). In fact, after-school hours among adolescents have been little studied (Lipsitz, 1986). Adolescents may be more or less supervised and "protected" in after-school activities, at home, or at part-time work (Greenberger and Steinberg, 1981). The comparative effects of participation in these activities require more study along with the effects of supervision for adolescents of different ages. Simmons and Blyth (1987) show that in the Milwaukee school system, early adolescent girls who participate more in extracurricular activities are somewhat more likely to be victimized by other students at school (presumably because the after-school hours in the school building are less supervised). In addition, junior high students who are allowed early freedom from parental supervision are more likely both to become victimized and to be involved in problem school behavior. (These findings persist when perceived maternal evaluation of the self is held constant. Thus, the negative effect of freedom from supervision does not appear to be a mere reflection of less parental love.) Although these findings require replication, they suggest that early adolescents may benefit from adult supervision in after-school hours.

In general, then, it appears important to distinguish overall school-wide factors from factors more proximate to the child (Epstein and Karweit, 1983; Entwisle and Hayduk, 1982; Anderson, 1982; Summers and Wolfe, 1977; Brookover and others, 1979). Figure 1 presents a potentially fruitful analytic model, along with an example derived from Epstein and Karweit (1983). All children are not exposed to the same set of experiences

Figure 1. Factors Affecting Adolescent Outcomes

School-Level ⟶ Structure and Climate	Proximate ⟶ Structure and Climate	Individual Outcomes
School size	Classroom organization	Friendship patterns
School differentation Age grading Tracking	Rank system	Self-image
	Visibility of one's skills	School problem behavior
	Extracurricular opportunity	

within the school, although the school-wide characteristics and policies constrain the likelihood of actual exposure to certain types of context. It is the particular exposure, along with the child's own characteristics, that are expected to affect individual outcomes. For instance, a very intelligent girl in a school that tracks students by math ability is likely to find herself in a mathematics classroom surrounded by other very intelligent youngsters and therefore may not have as high a self-image of her math aptitude as if she were in a more academically heterogeneous classroom (especially if the presence of tracking is kept a secret from the student body).

The process by which school factors have effects and the conditions under which such effects occur need more explication and study. For example, it would be valuable to investigate the ways in which school-wide and more proximate experiences affect the individual through normative reference group processes, modeling, processes of comparison (frog/pond effects) and interpersonal friendship and influence.

Rank in School. The psychosocial reaction to adolescent transitions, as noted above, depends not only on the outcome area at issue and the characteristics of the transition but also on the characteristics of the individuals. Thus, it is important to investigate whether certain types of children negotiate certain types of school transition better. One key characteristic of the child involves his or her rankings in school.

School is a context in which only a few children reach the highest levels of success. It is a context where many youngsters experience some level of failure, of comparatively low rank. Most children learn they are less good than some of their peers on the tasks highly valued by key adults. A sizable proportion learn they are poor at these tasks. While one method of dealing with failure is to withdraw from the situation, this method is defined as illegitimate until senior high. Thus, youngsters are compelled to spend a high proportion of their time in an environment in which adult authorities may be transmitting negative evaluations of them. The complex effects of this situation need to be better understood.

One reaction may be alienation from school. As children enter and move through adolescence and turn more to peers for evaluation, subgroups of children may unite and develop countercultures more favorable to themselves but more denigrating of school standards. Such counterculture groups may provide not only more favorable self-images but also intimacy in an impersonal environment. Antisocial behavior may be a part of this reaction.

Where children bring with them low social rank from the larger society into a heterogeneous school, the process can be more intense. Social class differences often permeate schools. Ogbu (n.d., p. 11, 16, 20) describes the counterculture of the underclass of black youths in a castelike stratification system in which blacks have been subordinated and where adult unemployment is high.

Although they verbalize a strong desire for education, black youths tend to behave in ways that will not necessarily lead to school success. . . .

Blacks also developed alternative or survival strategies. . . . Black youths know from observing their parents' situation . . . that their chances of making it through education and mainstream jobs are not very good. They therefore often become increasingly disillusioned . . . and consequently try less and less to do their schoolwork seriously.

Another type of response . . . is a deep distrust for the schools and white people who control them or their minority representatives. . . . Many potentially good students avoid doing their schoolwork seriously for fear of being accused by their peers of acting white.

If teachers show conscious or unconscious bias against such students, one would expect the long-term consequences to be more severe. If such children are segregated in different tracks within a school and/or excluded from academic and extracurricular reward structures, one might expect more subgroup conflict within the school. Clearly schools vary dramatically in the extent of intergroup conflict; the determinants and consequences of such conflict would benefit from further investigation. Also important are additional longitudinal studies of the causes and effects of school dropout for the mental health and behavior of these members of the "underclass."

Epstein and Karweit (1983) as well as Lipsitz (1984) emphasize the importance of multiple reward systems within a school. Multiple talents of children should be rewarded. According to Epstein and Karweit (1983) teachers should manage heterogeneous classrooms in such a way that cooperative behavior among high- and low-status youngsters is encouraged. They hypothesize that such cooperation will make the multiple talents of students visible to one another and prevent the academic rank structure from being the only salient basis for judgment in class. Alienation against academic prowess and against school conformity should be reduced in a school where there are many roads to success (Coleman, 1961).

Lipsitz (1984) also stresses the importance of equity of access to academic and extracurricular rewards for children from all backgrounds and concludes that equity and a high-quality education are not incompatible in the middle school years.

Concurrent Changes

School transition is only one of the transitions facing the early adolescent. An important issue is whether adolescent adjustment is affected by the cumulation or simultaneity of the multiple changes being experienced. One of the other major changes, of course, is that of pubertal development. Before turning to the question of the simultaneity of change, I wish to discuss some of the effects of pubertal timing itself. Since several other chapters in this volume deal with pubertal changes, only a few of the recent findings relevant to the social impact of pubertal timing during adolescence will be presented here.

Pubertal Timing. Much of the work in the area of pubertal changes has dealt with social asynchronies in development (see Eichorn, 1975; Dragastin, 1975). The issue here is the asynchrony between the individual's own level of physical development and that of his or her schoolmates. This is the problem of being on-time and off-time in one's life-course trajectory (see Elder, 1984, 1985). There has been a long history of studies comparing early, middle, and late developers (see Stolz and Stolz, 1951; Jones and Mussen, 1958; Faust, 1960; Mussen and Boutourline-Young, 1964; Dwyer and Mayer, 1968; Jones and others, 1971; MacFarlane, 1971; Clausen, 1975; Petersen and Taylor, 1980; Livson and Peskin, 1980; Apter and others, 1981; Savin-Williams, Small, and Zeldin, 1981; Brooks-Gunn and Petersen, 1983).

The major, early research was based on the California longitudinal studies (Jones and Mussen, 1958) and the Fels research (see Kagan and Moss, 1962; Moss and Kagan, 1972). From these studies, it was concluded that early pubertal development has positive short-term ramifications for boys but several negative effects for the girls (Mussen and Jones, 1958; Eichorn, 1963; Weatherley, 1964; Jones, 1965; Runyan, 1980; Comas, 1982). Long-terms effects, however, may be quite different (Peskin, 1973; Livson and Peskin, 1980; Haan, 1977).

These studies, of course, involve adolescents who grew up several decades ago. The major contemporary, large-scale, surveys of pubertal timing in the United States are the studies being conducted by Petersen and collaborators (Petersen, Tobin-Richards, and Boxer, 1983) and Duke, Gross, and Dornbusch (Dornbusch and others, 1981; Duke and others, 1982) and the author's own work (Simmons, Blyth, and McKinney, 1983; Blyth, Simmons, and Carlton-Ford, 1983; Simmons and Blyth, 1987). (See the two special issues of the *Journal of Youth and Adolescence* edited by Brooks-Gunn, Petersen, and Eichorn, 1985a, 1985b, for other very important research studies of pubertal development including work by Hill and others, 1985, and Brooks-Gunn, Petersen, and Eichorn, 1985a, 1985b, and Magnusson, Stattin, and Allen, 1985.)

Analyses from these studies suggest far fewer effects of pubertal timing than has customarily been assumed. Our own work shows no effects of pubertal timing on global self-esteem or on a wide variety of outcome measures. However, there is evidence that early developing boys have a more favorable body image (Tobin-Richards, Boxer, and Petersen,

1983; Duncan and others, 1985; Simmons and Blyth, 1987) and do better academically, while early-developing girls have less favorable body images (Brooks-Gunn and Petersen, 1983; Simmons, Blyth, and McKinney, 1983).

Particularly interesting from a social point of view is the evidence from Simmons and Blyth (1987) that early developers, both boys and girls, are likely to start dating earlier and to value opposite sex popularity more. It is unclear to what extent this difference is due to the fact that parents allow more freedom to children who look older, or to the greater attractiveness of more developed boys and girls to the opposite sex, or to their own higher levels of libido.

Also of great interest is evidence suggesting that early developing girls may be more likely to become involved in deviant or problem behavior. In the author's work (Simmons and Blyth, 1987), girls who have begun menstruating by sixth or seventh grade show more school behavior problems, are more likely to have been put on probation or suspension, and more likely to report skipping school in one or both of those years. Magnusson, Stattin, and Allen (1985) show similar relationships between early development and deviant behavior among girls in Sweden. The reason for this connection is not totally clear. Our data indicate that girls who look older are allowed more independence from parental supervision, and it is possible that this early independence allows them to become involved in deviant behavior. If so, we would have additional support for the developmental readiness hypothesis, the hypothesis that children can be thrust too soon into adolescence before they are ready for the rights and obligations of the new age period.

It is also possible that girls who are more developed than their peers are more likely to be tempted into deviant behavior because of differential peer-group interaction. More intense relationships with boys could be responsible, as could more relationships with older students. In fact, Magnusson, Stattin, and Allen (1985) show that more developed girls interact with older peer groups and that this interaction mediates the linkage to deviant behavior.

An additional hypothesis that could explain the relationship is that early developers find pubertal changes stressful, and this stress is reflected in their behavior. Finally, it is also conceivable that nonpubertal girls are compensating for their lack of popularity with the opposite sex by working hard in school and conforming to adult regulations. It should be noted that Jessor and Jessor (1977) show a linkage among problem behavior in general, early sexual relations, and a low GPA in school and Duncan and others (1985) show higher rates of deviant behavior among male, not female, early maturers in the United States.

This area is a fruitful one for additional research, both to make certain that the relationship between early puberty and deviant behavior among girls persists in future replications and, if so, to ascertain more of the reasons for the relationship.

Simultaneous Transitions (Cumulative Change). Of great relevance are the effects of cumulative change, that is, whether children find it more difficult to adjust to several changes simultaneously. In particular, are scheduled school transitions made more stressful if they occur at the same time as many other changes?

Relevant to this issue, Coleman (1974) has developed a focal theory of change. (Also see the author's work, Simmons and others, 1979.) According to this perspective, it is easier if the child goes through the various adolescent changes at different times rather than simultaneously. The focal model argues that gradual adjustment to one change before confrontation with another will be beneficial. That is, the ability to cope with the discontinuities created by major life transitions will be easier if they come into focus at different stages. Entry into adolescence involves changes in self-definition, in expectations by others, as well as in physical state and environmental context. Being able to tackle these issues one at a time will reduce the stresses inherent within the transitional process.

Some related work has been done in this area due to the extensive research on life events. (See reviews of this approach and its controversies by Zautra and Reich, 1983; Tausig, 1982; Newcomb, Huba, and Bentler, 1981; Pearlin and others, 1981; Kessler, 1979; Dohrenwend and Pearlin, 1981; Kessler, Price, and Wortman, 1985.) Relatively few studies in the life-events area, however, have dealt with normal early adolescents (see Gad and Johnson, 1980; Padilla, Rohsenow, and Bergman, 1976; Gersten and others, 1974, 1977; Newcomb, Huba, and Bentler, 1981; Johnson and McCutcheon, 1980; Swearingen and Cohen, 1985a, 1985b). Those few that have, by and large, do not concentrate on the normal, scheduled life-event changes of adolescence: the move into junior high, pubertal change, the onset of dating. (See Padilla's cross-sectional study of boys for an exception.) It should be noted that the Coddington Scale does include "Move into Junior High School" among its forty items (Coddington, 1972).

Thus, the focus of the life-event literature on nonnormative (nonscheduled) change is slightly different from the approach of Coleman (1974) and the author's. Coleman and I have been concerned with testing the idea that it is easier to cope with one normative (scheduled) life-course change at a time, rather than with many simultaneously. Like Elder and Rockwell (1979), we think the actual set of life changes have to be considered in the context of normative (socially expected) transitions in the life course.

In support of Coleman's focal theory of changes, I and my colleagues have recently shown that children who experience several major life changes at the same time experience more difficulty in terms of self-esteem, GPA, and extracurricular participation, and problem school behavior (Simmons and Blyth, 1987; Simmons and others, in press). Children in our longitudinal study were classified as to whether they had experienced major change in or prior to grade 7 entry in the following normative and nonnormative respects: (1) entry into a junior high school rather than remaining in K-8 school, (2) pubertal change close to grade 7 entry, (3) early onset of dating, (4) nonnormative geographical mobility since grade 6, and (5) major family disruption since age 9 (death, divorce, or remarriage of a parent).

Except for the change into junior high school, none of these changes in themselves affected subsequent self-esteem in grade 7. However, in combination there is certainly an effect on self-esteem. As the number of transitions increase, adjustment worsens not only for self-esteem but also for GPA, extracurricular participation, and problem behavior. Children who have experienced multiple changes can be identified as a group at risk. The differences between youngsters experiencing no changes and those experiencing four to five changes are sizable. In GPA the difference is an entire letter grade, from an average grade of B to an average of C. In terms of school extracurricular activities (clubs and sports), participation declines by more than one activity when the average number of activities overall is less than one at this age. For girls (only) self-esteem declines by one-half of a standard deviation unit. Problem behavior increases by 0.41 of a standard deviation unit for girls and 0.59 of a standard deviation unit for boys. In sum, the effects of multiple simultaneous changes are considerable and negative.

I have suggested that the idea of an "arena of comfort" is compatible with these findings. If changes come too suddenly, that is, if there is too much discontinuity with prior experience, or if change is too early given children's cognitive and emotional states, or if it occurs in too many areas of life at once, then individuals appear to experience considerable discomfort. Individuals appear to do better both in terms of self-esteem and behavioral coping if there is some arena of comfort in their lives.

If the adolescent is comfortable in some environments, life arenas, and role relationships, then discomfort in another arena can be tolerated and mastered. At entry to adolescence, children appear to be less able to cope if at one and the same time they are uncomfortable with their bodies (due to physical changes), with family (due to changes in family constellation), with home (because of a move), with school (due to great discontinuity in the nature of the school environment), with peers (because of the emergence of opposite sex relationships and because of the disruption of prior peer networks and the changes in peer expectations and peer evaluation criteria). It is likely that there needs to be some set of role relationships with which the individual can feel relaxed and comfortable, to which he or she can withdraw and become reinvigorated.

Of course, one presumes that for optimal self-esteem and coping in the long run, the individual cannot be totally comfortable; he or she has to leave the securities of childhood and enter adolescence. In an urban context, the individual should learn to cope with large-scale organizational environments with all their opportunities as well as their impersonality. The child has to detach emotionally and physically from parents and accept expectations from peers and parents more suitable for this new period in the life course (Elder, 1968). Physical changes are inevitable, and most youth will have to deal with the new type of romantic/sexual relationships.

Coping with all of these normative changes will necessarily involve some degree of discomfort, even if nonnormative and less desirable changes are absent. The issue that has been emphasized here involves timing and pacing. Gradual rather than discontinuous change, changes that are spread out and dealt with in turn, rather than simultaneously, appear recommended by these findings.

Conclusions

In this chapter, I have attempted to review the literature on the impact of the key social context of school and the effect of school transition on the child at entrance to adolescence. It is clear that transitions in adolescence are not universally problematic but that reaction depends on (1) characteristics of the transition, (2) characteristics of the individual, and (3) the outcome area at issue. I have hypothesized that transitions marked by great discontinuity and that move the child into an impersonal environment will be more difficult. Evidence has been presented to suggest that particular children who experience many life changes simultaneously are more at risk, as are children who are faced with early transitions before they are developmentally ready. In addition, different types of transitions have effects on different outcome areas, but overall one of the most problematic areas in adolescence is deviant behavior.

Several directions of future research appear recommended from this review. First of all, to what extent do youth of different ages benefit from protection versus challenge during in-school and after-school hours? In this light, more research into the effects of various alternative timings of school transitions at entry to adolescence could be fruitful. Do middle schools of various types present youngsters with a more gradual, less discontinuous, and less impersonal change and with a change that coincides less with other adolescent transitions? If there is evidence of benefit for children's adjustment, are these benefits short-term or long-lasting?

Furthermore, the factors that mitigate and aggravate adjustment to the various types of school transitions should be investigated in order that the relevant processes be better understood. Which personal resources help and which personal characteristics hinder adolescents as they change into various types of organizational context?

How do socially disadvantaged versus advantaged children cope with various types of transitions? Not only would it be beneficial to know which psychosocial characteristics of the child ease the adjustment to change, but also which specific structural and social features of the school are helpful. In particular, it would be valuable to determine which factors increase a sense of impersonality in the school, and whether the resultant impersonality hinders the ability of the adolescent to cope.

The general literature on response to stress emphasizes the importance of social support systems as buffers (Pearlin and others, 1981). Here we are suggesting more investigation of the changing social support networks of early and later adolescents. The importance of school structure and school transition in affecting friendship networks should be explored as well as the role of stable versus changing friendship networks on teenagers' behaviors and mental health.

The area of cumulative change should be a fruitful one for further investigation. Pubertal timing, one of the multiple transitions impacting on the adolescent, could be conceptualized in new ways in future research. Brooks-Gunn, Petersen, and Eichorn (1985a, 1985b) have emphasized the multidimensionality of pubertal change and the fact that different physical changes have different effects. In addition to the issue of whether the student is on-time or off-time in relation to peers along these various dimensions (an early, middle, or late developer), the effect of rate of pubertal development or tempo as described by Tanner (1987) could be studied. Do children who experience a greater amount of change in a given time find the transition to adolescence more difficult? Do those for whom the process is more gradual, less dramatic, and longer-lasting react more positively? In other words, pubertal change like school change can be more or less "discontinuous," and the question is whether greater discontinuity causes children more difficulty.

The developmental readiness hypothesis also promises a fruitful line of investigation—the idea that negative effects will be evident when youngsters are unprotected and are pushed too early into adolescent behavior. How do parental rules relative to early independence from supervision affect peer relationships, deviant behavior, and being exposed to situations where one might be victimized? More exploration of the negative and positive impact of interaction of pubertal and prepubertal children with older youth appears advised. At issue in general is the ideal balance between protection and challenge.

This chapter has emphasized the problems at entry to adolescence. But the effects of transition on the later adolescent are also relevant. To what extent do individuals recover from the problems encountered in early adolescence? To what extent do they respond the same way to both early and later life-changes? Again, longitudinal studies are recommended.

Finally, there is need for a variety of investigational styles including in-depth ethnographic work. Among these styles, there is a need for a certain number of large-scale, random-sample, investigations so that results can be generalized and so that individuals from different social locations can be compared. For example, in what ways does the process of entry to adolescence and the associated problems differ in urban, suburban, and rural contexts? In what ways are black and white youngsters affected differently by various types of school transitions, by cumulative change, and by pubertal timing? Almost all studies report great gender differences in reaction to adolescence, although investigators sometimes draw different conclusions. While Bronfenbrenner and Crouter (1983) argue that males are generally at greater risk, Simmons and Blyth (1987) show more negative reactions to school and pubertal transitions among girls. It is important in future research to identify major differences in the ways males and females, and youngsters from different social backgrounds and geographical locales react to adolescent transition.

As a period in the life course, adolescence allows investigation of the interactions of biological, psychological, and social structural conditions as they affect mental health and social behavior. The resultant interdisciplinary emphasis should continue to yield a richness of important research.

References

Alexander, K. L., McPartland, J. M., and Cook, M. A. "Using Standardized Test Performance in School Effects Research." *Research in Sociology of Education and Socialization*, 1981, *2*, 1-33.

Alwin, D. F., and Otto, L. B. "High School Context Effects on Aspirations." *Sociology of Education*, 1977, *50*, 259-273.

Anderson, C. S. "The Search for School Climate: A Review of the Research." *Review of Educational Research*, 1982, *52* (3), 368-420.

Apter, A., Galatzer, A., Beth-Halachmi, N., and Laron, Z. "Self-Image in Adolescents with Delayed Pubertal and Growth Retardation." *Journal of Youth and Adolescence*, 1981, *10*, 501-505.

Attenborough, R. E., and Zdep, S. M. "Self-Image Among a National Probability Sample of Girls." *Proceedings*, of the Eighty-First Annual Convention, American Psychological Association, 1973, 237-238.

Bachman, J. G., and O'Malley, P. M. "The Search for School Effects: Some New Findings and Perspectives." Unpublished manuscript. Ann Arbor, Mich.: Institute for Social Research, 1980.

Bachman, J. G., O'Malley, P. M., and Johnston, J. "Adolescent to Adulthood: Change and Stability in the Lives of Young Men." *Youth in Transition*. Vol. 6. Ann Arbor, Mich.: Institute for Social Research, 1978.

Bandura, A. "The Stormy Decade: Fact or Fiction?" In D. Rogers (ed.), *Issues in Adolescent Psychology*. (2nd ed.) New York: Appleton-Century-Crofts, 1972.

Barglow, P., and Schaefer, M. "The Fate of the Feminine Self in Normative Adolescent Regression." In M. Sugar (ed.), *Female Adolescent Development*. New York: Brunner/Mazel, 1979.

Barker, R. C., and Gump, P. V. "Big School—Small School: Studies of the Effects of High School Size on the Behavior and Experiences of Students." Topeka: Midwest Psychological Field Station, University of Kansas, 1962.

Benedict, R. "Continuities and Discontinuities in Cultural Conditioning." In W. E. Martin and C. B. Stendler (eds.), *Readings in Child Development*. New York: Harcourt Brace Jovanovich, 1954.

Berkovitz, I. H. "Effects of Secondary School Experiences on Adolescent Female Development." In M. Sugar (ed.), *Female Adolescent Development*. New York: Brunner/Mazel, 1979.

Bidwell, C. E., and Kasarda, J. D. "Conceptualizing and Measuring the Effects of School and Schooling." *American Journal of Education*, 1980, *88*, 401-430.

Black, D. "Crime as Social Control." *American Sociological Review*, 1983, *48*, 34-45.

Blos, P. *On Adolescence: A Psychoanalytic Interpretation*. New York: Free Press, 1962.

Blos P. "The Child Analyst Looks at the Young Adolescent." *Daedalus*, 1971, *100*, 961-978.

Blumstein, A., Farrington, D. P., and Moitra, S. "Delinquency Careers: Innocents, Desisters, and Persisters." In M. Tonry and N. Morris (eds.), *Crime and Justice, An Annual Review of Research*. Vol. 6. Chicago: University of Chicago Press, 1985.

Blyth, D. A., Hill, J. P., and Smyth, C. K. "The Influence of Older Adolescents on Younger Adolescents: Do Grade-Level Arrangements Make a Difference in Behaviors, Attitudes, and Experiences?" *Journal of Early Adolescence*, 1981, 1 *(1)*, 85-110.

Blyth, D. A., and Karnes, E. L. *Philosophy, Policies, and Programs for Early Adolescent Education: An Annotated Bibliography*. Westport, Conn.: Greenwood, 1981.

Blyth, D. A., Simmons, R. G., and Carlton-Ford, S. "The Adjustment of Early Adolescents to School Transitions." *Journal of Early Adolescence*, 1983, *3* (1 and 2), 105-120.

Boesel, D., Crain, R., Dunteman, G., Ianni, F., Martinolich, M., Moles, O., Spivak, H., Stalford, C., and Wayne, I. *Violent Schools—Safe Schools: The Safe School Study Report to the Congress*. Vol. 1. U.S. Department of Health, Education, and Welfare, National Institute of Education. Washington, D.C.: U.S. Government Printing Office, 1978.

Bohan, J. S. "Age and Sex Differences in Self-Concept." *Adolescence*, 1973, *8*, 379-384.

Bowman, D. O. "A Longitudinal Study of Selected Facets of Children's Self-Concepts as Related to Achievement and Intelligence." *The Citadel: Monograph Series*, no. 22. 1974, 1-16.

Bronfenbrenner, U. *Two Worlds of Childhood: U.S. and U.S.S.R.* New York: Russell Sage Foundation, 1970.

Bronfenbrenner, U., and Crouter, A. C. "The Evolution of Environmental Models in Developmental Research." In W. P. Kensen (ed.), *History, Theory, and Methods*. Vol. 1. *Handbook of Child Psychology*. (4th ed.). New York: Wiley, 1983.

Brookover, W., Beady, C., Flood, P., Schweitzer, J., and Wisenbaker, J. *School Social Systems and Student Achievement: Schools Can Make a Difference*. New York: Praeger, 1979.

Brooks-Gunn, J., and Petersen, A. C. (eds.). *Girls at Puberty: Biological and Psychosocial Perspectives*. New York: Plenum, 1983.

Brooks-Gunn, J., Petersen, A. C., and Eichorn, D. (eds.). *Journal of Youth and Adolescence*, 1985a, *14* (3), entire issue.

Brooks-Gunn, J., Petersen, A. C., and Eichorn, D. (eds.). *Journal of Youth and Adolescence*, 1985b, *14* (4), entire issue.

Carlson, R. "Stability and Change in the Adolescent's Self-Image." *Child Development*, 1965, *35*, 659–666.

Clausen, J. A. "The Social Meaning of Differential Physical and Sexual Maturation." In S. E. Dragastin and G. H. Elder, Jr. (eds.), *Adolescence in the Life Cycle: Psychological Change and Social Context*. New York: Wiley, 1975.

Coddington, R. D. "The Significance of Life Events as Etiologic Factors in the Diseases of Children." *Journal of Psychosomatic Research*, 1972, *16*, 7–18.

Coleman, J. C. *Relationships in Adolescence*. Boston: Routledge & Kegan Paul, 1974.

Coleman, J. S. *The Adolescent Society*. New York: Free Press, 1961.

Coleman, J. S., Campbell, E. Q., Hobson, C. J., McPartland, J., Mood, A. M., Weinfeld, F. D., and York, R. L. *Equality of Educational Opportunity*. Washington, D.C.: U.S. Government Printing Office, 1966.

Comas, J. M. "Personality Characteristics of Eighteen- to Twenty-Two-Year-Old Adolescent Males Self-Rated as Early, Average, and Late Physical Maturers." *Dissertation Abstracts International*, 1982, 3870-A.

Dohrenwend, B. P., and Pearlin, L. I. "Report of the Panel on Life Events from the Committee for Research on Stress in Health and Disease." Washington, D.C.: Institute of Medicine, National Academy of Sciences, 1981.

Dornbusch, S. M., Carlsmith, J. M., Gross, R. T., Martin, J. A., Jennings, D., Rosenberg, A., and Duke, P. "Sexual Development, Age, and Dating: A Comparison of Biological and Social Influences on One Set of Behaviors." *Child Development*, 1981, *52*, 179–185.

Douvan, E., and Adelson, J. *The Adolescent Experience*. New York: Wiley, 1966.

Dragastin, S. "Research Themes and Priorities." In S. Dragastin and G. H. Elder, Jr. (eds.), *Adolescence in the Life Cycle*. New York: Wiley, 1975.

Duke, P. M., Carlsmith, J. M., Jennings, D., Martin, J. A., Dornbusch, S. M., Siegel-Gorelick, B., and Gross, R. T. "Educational Correlates of Early and Late Sexual Maturation in Adolescence." *Journal of Pediatrics*, 1982, *100* (4), 633–637.

Duncan, P. D., Ritter, P. L., Dornbusch, S. M., Gross, R. T., and Carlsmith, J. M. "The Effects of Pubertal Timing on Body Image, School Behavior, and Deviance." *Journal of Youth and Adolescence*, 1985, *14* (3), 236–277.

Dusek, J. B., and Flaherty, J. F. "The Development of the Self-Concept During the Adolescent Years." *Monographs of the Society for Research in Child Development*, 1981, *46* (4), entire issue.

Dwyer, J., and Mayer, J. "Psychological Effects of Variations in Physical Appearance During Adolescence." *Adolescence*, 1968, *3*, 353–380.

Eccles, J. S. "Do Students Turn Off to Math in Junior High School?" Paper presented in conjunction with a symposium entitled "Early Adolescence: Attitudinal and Environmental Changes," at the annual meeting of the American Educational Research Association, New Orleans, April 1984.

Eccles, J. S., Midgley, C., and Adler, T. F. "Grade-Related Changes in School Environment: Effects on Achievement Motivation." In J. G. Nichols (ed.), *Advances in Motivation and Achievement: The Development of Achievement Motivation*. Vol. 3. Greenwich, Conn.: JAI, 1984.

Eichorn, D. H. "Biological Correlates of Behavior." In H. W. Stevenson (ed.), *Child Psychology*. Part 1. Chicago: University of Chicago Press, 1963.

Eichorn, D. H. "Asynchronizations in Adolescent Development." In S. E. Dragastin and G. H. Elder, Jr. (eds.), *Adolescence and the Life Cycle*. New York: Halsted, 1975.

Elder, G. H., Jr. "Adolescent Socialization and Development." In E. F. Borgatta and W. W. Lambert (eds.), *Handbook of Personality Theory and Research*. Chicago: Rand McNally, 1968.

54

Elder, G. H., Jr. "Families, Kin, and the Life Course: A Sociological Perspective." In R. Parke (ed.), *Advances in Child Development Research*. Vol. 7. *The Family*. Chicago: University of Chicago Press, 1984.

Elder, G. H., Jr. (ed.). *Life Course Dynamics: Trajectories and Transitions, 1968-1980*. Ithaca, N.Y.: Cornell University Press, 1985.

Elder, G. H., Jr., and Rockwell, R. C. "The Life Course and Human Development: An Ecological Perspective." *International Journal of Behavioral Development*, 1979, *2*, 1-21.

Elkind, D. "Egocentrism in Adolescence." *Child Development*, 1967, *38*, 1025-1034.

Elkind, D. *All Grown Up and No Place to Go: Teenagers in Crisis*. Reading, Mass.: Addison-Wesley, 1984.

Elliott, D. S., Huizinga, D., and Ageton, S. S. "Delinquency and Drug Use Self-Report Scale Developed for the National Youth Survey." In D. S. Elliott (ed.), *Explaining Delinquency and Drug Use*. Newbury Park, Calif.: Sage, 1985.

Engel, M. "The Stability of the Self-Concept in Adolescence." *Journal of Abnormal and Social Psychology*, 1959, *58*, 211-215.

Entwisle, D. R., and Hayduk, L. A. *Early Schooling: Cognitive and Affective Outcomes*. Baltimore: Johns Hopkins University Press, 1982.

Epstein, J. L., and Karweit, N. *Friends in School: Patterns of Selection and Influence in Secondary Schools*. Orlando, Fla.: Academic Press, 1983.

Epstein, J. L., and McPartland, J. M. "The Concept and Measurement of the Quality of School Life." *American Educational Research Journal*, 1976, *13*, 15-30.

Erikson, E. H. "Identity and the Life Cycle." *Psychological Issues*, 1959, *1*, 1-171.

Erikson, E. H. *Identity: Youth and Crisis*. New York: Norton, 1968.

Faust, M. S. "Development Maturity as a Determinant in Prestige of Adolescent Girls." *Child Development*, 1960, *31*, 173-184.

Felner, R. D., Ginter, M., and Primavera, J. "Primary Prevention During School Transitions: Social Support and Environmental Structure." *American Journal of Community Psychology*, 1982, *10* (3), 277-290.

Felner, R. D., Primavera, J., and Cauce, A. M. "The Impact of School Transitions: A Focus for Preventive Efforts." *American Journal of Community Psychology*, 1981, *9* (4), 449-459.

Flanagan, J. C., Dailey, J. T., Shaycoft, M. F., Orr, D. B., and Goldberg, I. *Studies of the American High School*. Pittsburgh, Pa.: Project Talent Office, University of Pittsburgh, 1962.

Freud, A. "Adolescence." *Psychoanalytic Study of the Child*, 1958, *13*, 255-278.

Gad, M. T., and Johnson, J. H. "Correlates of Adolescent Life Stress as Related to Race, Sex, and Levels of Perceived Social Support." *Journal of Clinical Child Psychology*, Spring 1980, 13-16.

Gersten, J. C., Langner, T. S., Eisenberg, J. G., and Orzeck, L. "Child Behavior and Life Events: Undesirable Change or Change Per Se?" In B. S. Dohrenwend and B. P. Dohrenwend (eds.), *Stressful Life Events: Their Nature and Effects*. New York: Wiley, 1974.

Gersten, J. C., Langner, T. S., Eisenberg, J. G., and Simcha-Fagan, O. "An Evaluation of the Etiologic Role of Stressful Life-Change Events in Psychological Disorders." *Journal of Health and Social Behavior*, 1977, *18*, 228-244.

Glaser, B. G., and Strauss, A. L. *Status Passage*. Chicago: Aldine-Atherton, 1971.

Gove, W. R. "The Effect of Age and Gender on Deviant Behavior: A Biopsychosocial Perspective." In A. S. Rossi (ed.), *Gender and the Life Course*. New York: Aldine, 1985.

Greenberger, E., and Steinberg, L. "The Workplace as a Context for the Socialization of Youth." *Journal of Youth and Adolescence*, 1981, *10*, 185-210.

Grinker, R., Grinker, R., and Timberlake, J. "A Study of Mentally Healthy Young Males (Homoclites)." *American Medical Association Archives of General Psychiatry*, 1962, *6*, 405–453.

Haan, N. *Coping and Defending: Process of Self-Environment Organization.* Orlando, Fla.: Academic Press, 1977.

Hall, G. S. *Adolescence: Its Psychology and Its Relations to Physiology, Anthropology, Sociology, Sex, Crime, Religion and Education.* New York: Appleton, 1904.

Hamburg, B. A. "Early Adolescence: A Specific and Stressful Stage of the Life Cycle." In G. V. Coelho, D. A. Hamburg, and J. E. Adams (eds.), *Coping and Adaptation.* New York: Basic Books, 1974.

Harris, D. A. "A Comparative Study of Selected Middle Schools and Selected Junior High Schools." Unpublished Ph.D. dissertation, Ball State University, Muncie, Indiana, 1968.

Harter, S. "The Perceived Competence Scale for Children." *Child Development*, 1982, *53*, 87–97.

Hauser, R. M., Sewell, W. H., and Alwin, D. F. "High School Effects on Achievement." In W. H. Sewell, R. M. Hauser, and D. L. Featherman (eds.), *Schooling and Achievement in American Society.* Orlando, Fla.: Academic Press, 1976.

Hawkins, J., and Berndt, T. J. "Adjustment Following the Transition to Junior High School." Paper presented at the Biennial Meeting of the Society for Research in Child Development, Toronto, Canada, 1985.

Hill, J. P., Holmbeck, G. N., Marlow, L., Green, T. M., and Lynch, M. E. "Menarcheal Status and Parent-Child Relations in Families of Seventh-Grade Girls." *Journal of Youth and Adolescence*, 1985, *14* (4), 301–316.

Jessor, R. "The Stability of Change: Psychosocial Development from Adolescence to Young Adulthood." In D. Magnusson and V. Allen (eds.), *Human Development: An Interactional Perspective.* Orlando, Fla.: Academic Press, 1983.

Jessor, R., and Jessor, S. L. *Problem Behavior and Psychological Development: A Longitudinal Study of Youth.* Orlando, Fla.: Academic Press, 1977.

Johnson, J. H., and McCutcheon, S. "Assessing Life Events in Older Children and Adolescents: Preliminary Findings with the Life Event Checklist." In I. G. Sarason and C. D. Spielberger (eds.), *Stress and Anxiety.* Washington, D.C.: Hemisphere, 1980.

Johnson, R. E. *Juvenile Delinquency and Its Origins.* Cambridge, Mass.: Cambridge University Press, 1979.

Johnston, L. "The American High School." Working paper, no. 9. Ann Arbor, Mich.: University of Michigan, Institute of Social Research, 1973.

Jones, M. C. "Psychological Correlates of Somatic Development." *Child Development*, 1965, *36*, 899–911.

Jones, M. C., Bayley, N., MacFarlane, J. W., and Honzik, M. (eds.). *The Course of Human Development.* Waltham, Mass.: Xerox College Publishing, 1971.

Jones, M. C., and Mussen, P. H. "Self-Conceptions and Interpersonal Attitudes of Early- and Late-Maturing Girls." *Child Development*, 1958, *29*, 491–501.

Jorgensen, E. C., and Howell, R. J. "Changes in Self, Ideal-Self Correlations from Ages 3 Through 18." *The Journal of Social Psychology*, 1969, *79*, 63–67.

Kagan, J., and Moss, H. A. *Birth to Maturity: A Study in Psychological Development.* New York: Wiley, 1962.

Kandel, D. B. "Drug and Drinking Behavior Among Youth." *Annual Review of Sociology*, 1980, *6*, 235–285.

Kaplan, H. B. "The Self-Esteem Motive and Change in Self-Attitudes." *Journal of Nervous and Mental Disease*, 1975, *161*, 265–275.

Karweit, N., and Hansell, S. "School Organization and Friendship Selection." In

J. L. Epstein and N. Karweit (eds.), *Friends in School: Patterns of Selection and Influence in Secondary Schools.* Orlando, Fla.: Academic Press, 1983.

Katz, P., and Zigler, E. "Self-Image Disparity: A Developmental Approach." *Journal of Personality and Social Psychology,* 1967, *5* (2), 186–195.

Kessler, R. C. "A Strategy for Studying Differential Vulnerability to the Psychological Consequences of Stress." *Journal of Health and Social Behavior,* 1979, *20,* 100–108.

Kessler, R. C., Price, R. H., and Wortman, C. B. "Social Factors in Psychopathology: Stress, Social Support, and Coping Processes." *Annual Review of Psychology,* 1985, *36,* 531–572.

Lightfoot, S. L. *The Good High School: Portraits of Character and Culture.* New York: Basic Books, 1983.

Lipsitz, J. *Growing Up Forgotten.* Lexington, Mass.: Lexington Books, 1977.

Lipsitz, J. *Successful Schools for Young Adolescents.* New Brunswick, N.J.: Transaction Books, 1984.

Lipsitz, J. "School Improvement and Out-of-School Learning: Making the Connection." Paper presented at the First Biennial Meeting, Society for Research on Adolescence, Madison, Wisconsin, 1986.

Livson, N., and Peskin, H. "Perspectives on Adolescence from Longitudinal Research." In J. Adelson (ed.), *Handbook of Adolescent Psychology.* New York: Wiley, 1980.

McCaig, T. E. "The Differential Influence of the Junior High School and Elementary School Organizational Patterns on Academic Achievement and Social Adjustment of Seventh and Eighth Grade Students." Unpublished Ph.D. dissertation, Loyola University, 1967.

McCarthy, J. D., and Hoge, D. R. "Analysis of Age Effects in Longitudinal Studies of Adolescent Self-Esteem." *Developmental Psychology,* 1982, *18* (3), 372–379.

McDill, E. L., and Rigsby, L. C. *Structure and Process in Secondary Schools: The Academic Impact of Educational Climates.* Baltimore, Md.: Johns Hopkins University Press, 1973.

MacFarlane, J. W. "The Impact of Early and Late Maturation in Boys and Girls: Illustrations from Life Records of Individuals." In M. C. Jones, N. Bayley, J. W. MacFarlane, and M. Honzik (eds.), *The Course of Human Development.* Waltham, Mass.: Xerox College Publishing, 1971.

Magnusson, D., Stattin, H., and Allen, V. L. "Biological Maturation and Social Development: A Longitudinal Study of Some Adjustment Processes from Mid-Adolescence to Adulthood." *Journal of Youth and Adolescence,* 1985, *14* (4), 267–284.

Metcalfe, B.M.A. "Self-Concept and Attitude to School." *British Journal of Educational Psychology,* 1981, *51,* 66–76.

Monge, R. H. "Developmental Trends in Factors of Adolescent Self-Concept." *Developmental Psychology,* 1973, *8,* 382–392.

Mooney, P. "A Comparative Study of Achievement and Attendance of Ten- to Fourteen-Year-Olds in a Middle School and Other School Organizations." Unpublished Ph.D. dissertation, University of Florida, Gainesville, 1970.

Morgan, D. L., and Alwin, D. F. "When Less Is More: School Size and Student Social Participation." *Social Psychology Quarterly,* 1980, *43* (2), 241–252.

Moriarty, A., and Toussieng, P. "Adolescence in a Time of Transition." *Bulletin of the Menninger Clinic,* 1975, *39,* 391–408.

Moss, H. A., and Kagan, J. "Report on Personality Consistency and Change from the Fels Longitudinal Study." In D. R. Heise (ed.), *Personality and Socialization.* Chicago: Rand McNally, 1972.

Mussen, P. H., and Boutourline-Young, H. "Relationships Between Rate of Physical Maturing and Personality Among Boys of Italian Descent." *Vita Humana,* 1964, *7,* 186–200.

Mussen, P. H., and Jones, M. C. "The Behavior-Inferred Motivations of Late- and Early-Maturing Boys." *Child Development,* 1958, *29,* 61–67.

Newcomb, M. D., Huba, G. J., and Bentler, P. M. "A Multidimensional Assessment of Stressful Life Events Among Adolescents: Derivation and Correlates." *Journal of Health Social Behavior,* 1981, *22,* 400–415.

Offer, D. *The Psychological World of the Teenager: A Study of Normal Adolescent Boys.* New York: Basic Books, 1969.

Offer, D., and Offer, J. *From Teenage to Young Manhood: A Psychological Study.* New York: Basic Books, 1975.

Offer, D., Ostrove, E., and Howard, K. I. *The Adolescent: A Psychological Self-Portrait.* New York: Basic Books, 1981.

Ogbu, J. U. "Cultural Discontinuities and Schooling." *Anthropology and Education Quarterly,* 1982, *13* (4), 290–307.

Ogbu, J. U. "Class Stratification, Racial Stratification, and Schooling." Unpublished manuscript, University of California, Berkeley, n.d.

O'Malley, P. M., and Bachman, J. G. "Self-Esteem: Change and Stability Between Ages 13 and 23." *Developmental Psychology,* 1983, *19* (2), 257–268.

Padilla, E. R., Rohsenow, D. J., and Bergman, A. B. "Predicting Accident Frequency in Children." *Pediatrics,* 1976, *58,* 223–226.

Pearlin, L. I., Lieberman, M. A., Menaghan, E. G., and Mullan, J. T. "The Stress Process." *Journal of Health and Social Behavior,* 1981, *22,* 337–356.

Peskin, H. "Influence of the Developmental Schedule of Puberty on Learning and Ego Development." *Journal of Youth and Adolescence,* 1973, *2,* 273–290.

Petersen, A. C. "Pubertal Change and Cognition." In J. Brooks-Gunn and A. C. Petersen (eds.), *Girls at Puberty.* New York: Plenum, 1983.

Petersen, A. C., and Taylor, B. "The Biological Approach to Adolescence: Biological Change and Psychological Adaptation." In J. Adelson (ed.), *Handbook of Adolescent Psychology.* New York: Wiley, 1980.

Petersen, A. C., Tobin-Richards, M., and Boxer, A. "Puberty: Its Measurement and Its Meaning." *Journal of Early Adolescence,* 1983, *3* (1 and 2), 47–62.

Piers, E. V., and Harris, D. B. "Age and Other Correlates of Self-Concept in Children." *Journal of Educational Psychology,* 1964, *55* (2), 91–95.

Protinsky, H., and Farrier, S. "Self-Image Changes in Pre-Adolescents and Adolescents." *Adolescence,* 1980, *15* (6), 887–893.

Purkey, S. C., and Smith, M. S. "Effective Schools: A Review." *The Elementary School Journal,* 1983, *83* (4), 427–452.

Ramsøy, N. R. "American High Schools at Mid-Century." Unpublished report, Bureau of Applied Social Research, Columbia University, 1961.

Rankin, H. J. "A Study of the Pre- and Post-Attitudes and Academic Achievements of Students in Grades 5 Through 10 in a Change from a Junior High Organization to a Middle School Organization in a Suburban School System." Unpublished Ph.D. dissertation, Syracuse University, Syracuse, New York, 1969.

Reid, L. D. "Year of School Transition and Its Effects on Students." Unpublished Ph.D. dissertation, University of Minnesota, 1983.

Reuman, D. "Consequences of the Transition into Junior High School on Social Comparison of Abilities and Achievement Motivation." Paper presented at the annual meeting of the American Educational Research Association, New Orleans, April 1984.

Rowan, B., Bossert, S. T., and Dwyer, D. C. "Research on Effective Schools: A Cautionary Note." *Educational Researcher,* 1983, *12,* 24-31.

Runyan, W. M. "The Life Satisfaction Chart: Perceptions of the Course of Subjective Experience." *International Journal of Aging and Human Development,* 1980, *11,* 45-64.

Rutter, M., and Giller, H. *Juvenile Delinquency Trends and Perspectives.* New York: Guilford, 1984.

Rutter, M., Maughan, B., Mortimore, P., and Ouston, J., with Smith, A. *Fifteen Thousand Hours: Secondary Schools and Their Effects on Children.* Cambridge, Mass.: Harvard University Press, 1979.

Savin-Williams, R. C., and Demo, D. H. "Developmental Change and Stability in Adolescent Self-Concept." *Developmental Psychology,* 1984, *20* (6), 1100-1110.

Savin-Williams, R. C., Small, S. A., and Zeldin, R. S. "Dominance and Altruism Among Adolescent Males: A Comparison of Ethological and Psychological Methods." *Ethology and Sociobiology,* 1981, *2,* 167-176.

Schoo, P. H. "Students' Self-Concepts, Social Behavior, and Attitudes Toward School in Middle and Junior High Schools." Unpublished Ph.D. dissertation, University of Michigan, 1970.

Simmons, R. G., and Blyth, D. A. *Moving into Adolescence: The Impact of Pubertal Change and School Context.* Hawthorne, N.Y.: Aldine, 1987.

Simmons, R. G., Blyth, D. A., and McKinney, K. L. "The Social and Psychological Effects of Puberty on White Females." In J. Brooks-Gunn and A. Petersen, (eds.), *Girls at Puberty: Biological and Psychosocial Perspectives.* New York: Plenum, 1983.

Simmons, R. G., Blyth, D. A., Van Cleave, E. F., and Bush, D. M. "Entry into Early Adolescence: The Impact of School Structure, Puberty, and Early Dating on Self-Esteem." *American Sociological Review,* 1979, *44* (6), 948-967.

Simmons, R. G., Burgeson, R., Carlton-Ford, S., and Blyth, D. A. "Reaction to the Cumulation of Change in Early Adolescence." In H. Stevenson and D. R. Entwisle (eds.), *Child Development,* in press.

Simmons, R. G., Rosenberg, M., and Rosenberg, F. "Disturbance in the Self-Image at Adolescence." *American Sociological Review,* 1973, *39* (5), 553-568.

Soares, L. M., and Soares, A. T. "Self-Concepts of Disadvantaged and Advantaged Students." *Proceedings,* Seventy-Eighth Annual Convention, American Psychological Association, 1970.

Sørenson, A. B., and Hallinan, M. T. "A Reconceptualization of School, Effects." *Sociology of Education,* 1977, *50,* 273-289.

Steinberg, L. D., and Hill, J. "Patterns of Family Interaction as a Function of Age, the Onset of Puberty, and Formal Thinking." *Developmental Psychology,* 1978, *14,* 683-684.

Stolz, H. R., and Stolz, L. M. *Somatic Development of Adolescent Boys.* New York: Macmillan, 1951.

Summers, A. A., and Wolfe, B. L. "Do Schools Make a Difference?" *The American Economic Review,* 1977, *67,* 639-652.

Swearingen, E. M., and Cohen, L. H. "Life Events and Psychological Distress: A Prospective Study of Young Adolescents." *Developmental Psychology,* 1985a, *21* (6), 1045-1054.

Swearingen, E. M., and Cohen, L. H. "Measurement of Adolescents' Life Events: The Junior High Life Experiences Survey." *American Journal of Community Psychology,* 1985b, *13* (1), 69-85.

Tanner, J. "Issues and Advances in Adolescent Growth and Development." *Journal of Adolescent Health Care,* 1987, *8* (6).

Tausig, M. "Measuring Life Events." *Journal of Health and Social Behavior*, 1982, *23*, 52-64.

Tobin-Richards, M. H., Boxer, A. M., and Petersen, A. C. "The Psychological Significance of Pubertal Change: Sex Differences in Perceptions of Self During Early Adolescence." In J. Brooks-Gunn and A. C. Petersen (eds.), *Girls at Puberty*. New York: Plenum, 1983.

Toennies, F. *Femeinschaft un Gesellschaft. [Fundamental Concepts of Sociology.]* New York: American Book, 1940. (Originally published 1887.)

Trowbridge, N. "Self-Concept and Socioeconomic Status in Elementary School Children." *American Educational Research Journal*, 1972, *9* (4), 525-537.

Weatherly, D. "Self-Perceived Rate of Physical Maturation and Personality in Late Adolescence." *Child Development*, 1964, *35*, 1197-1210.

Weiner, I. *Psychological Disturbance in Adolescence*. New York: Wiley-Interscience, 1970.

Wood, F. H. "A Comparison of Student Attitudes in Junior High and Middle Schools." *High School Journal*, 1973, *56*, 355-361.

Wylie, R. *The Self-Concept Theory and Research*. Vol. 2. (rev. ed.) Lincoln: University of Nebraska Press, 1979.

Yamamoto, K., Thomas, E. C., and Karns, E. A. "School-Related Attitudes in Middle-School Age Students." *American Educational Research Journal*, 1969, *6* (2), 191-206.

Zautra, A. J., and Reich, J. W. "Life Events and Perceptions of Life Quality: Developments in a Two-Factor Approach." *Journal of Community Psychology*, 1983, *11*, 121-132.

Further Sources

Alwin, D. F. "Social Contextual Effects." *Sociology of Education*, 1976, *49*, 294-303.

Bachman, J. G., and O'Malley, P. M. "Self-Esteem in Young Men: A Longitudinal Analysis of the Impact of Educational and Occupational Attainment." *Journal of Personality and Social Psychology*, 1977, *35*, 365-380.

Bachman, J. G., and O'Malley, P. M. "The Youth in Transition Series: A Study of Change and Stability in Young Men." In A. Kerchoff (ed.), *Research in Sociology of Education and Socialization*. Vol. 1. Greenwich, Conn.: JAI, 1980.

Blyth, D. A. *Continuities and Discontinuities During the Transition into Adolescence: A Longitudinal Comparison of Two School Structures*. Unpublished Ph.D. dissertation, University of Minnesota, 1977.

Brooks-Gunn, J., and Warren, M. P. "The Effects of Delayed Menarache in Different Contexts: Dance and Nondance Students." *Journal of Youth and Adolescence*, 1985, *14* (4), 285-300.

Coleman, J. S., Hoffer, T., and Kilgore, S. *High School Achievement: Public, Catholic, and Private Schools Compared*. New York: Basic Books, 1982.

Davis, A. "Socialization and Adolescent Personality." *Adolescence*, 1944, *43*, part 1.

Eckland, B. K., and Alexander, K. L. "The National Longitudinal Study of the High School Senior Class of 1972." In A. C. Kerckhoff (ed.), *Research in Sociology of Education and Socialization*. Vol. 1. Greenwich, Conn.: JAI, 1980.

Educational Research Service. *Organization of the Middle Grades: A Summary of Research*. Arlington, Va.: Educational Research Service, 1983.

Elder, G. H., Jr. *Children of the Great Depression*. Chicago: University of Chicago Press, 1974.

Elliott, D. S., Ageton, S. S., Huizinga, D., Knowles, B., and Canker, R. J. "The Prevalence and Incidence of Delinquent Behavior: 1976-1980." The National

Youth Survey Report, no. 26. Boulder, Colo.: Behavioral Research Institute, 1983.

Epps, E. G., and Smith, S. F. "School and Children: The Middle Childhood Years." In W. A. Collins (ed.), *Development During Middle Childhood, the Years from Six to Twelve*. Washington, D.C.: National Academy Press, 1984.

Epstein, J. L., and McPartland, J. M. "Authority Structure." In H. J. Walberg (ed.), *Educational Environments and Effects*. Berkeley, Calif.: McCutchan, 1979.

Feldlaufer, H. "Assessing Changes in Elementary and Junior High School Environments Using Observers' Reports." Paper presented as part of a symposium entitled "Early Adolescence: Attitudinal and Environmental Changes" at the American Educational Research Association Annual Meeting, New Orleans, April 1984.

Friedenberg, E. Z. *The Vanishing Adolescent*. Boston: Beacon Press, 1959.

Garnier, M. A., and Hout, M. "Schooling Processes and Educational Outcomes in France." *Quality and Quantity*, 1981, *15*, 151-177.

Gatewood, T. E. "What Research Says About the Junior High Versus the Middle School." *North Central Association Quarterly*, 1971, *46* (2), 264-276.

Gottfredson, G. D., and Daiger, D. C. *Disruption in Six Hundred Schools*. Baltimore, Md.: Center for Social Organization of Schools, Johns Hopkins University, 1979.

Gottfredson, G. D., Joffe, R. D., and Gottfredson, D. C. *Measuring Victimization and the Explanation of School Disruption*. Baltimore, Md.: Center for Social Organization of Schools, Johns Hopkins University, 1981.

Greenberg, D. F. "Delinquency and the Age Structure of Society." In D. F. Greenberg (ed.), *Crime and Capitalism*. Palo Alto, Calif.: Mayfield, 1981.

Hallinan, M. T. "Commentary, New Directors for Research on Peer Influence." In J. L. Epstein and N. Karweit (eds.), *Friends in School: Patterns of Selection and Influence in Secondary Schools*. Orlando, Fla.: Academic Press, 1983.

Hathaway, S. R., and Monachesi, E. D. *Adolescent Personality and Behavior: MMPI Patterns*. Minneapolis: University Press, 1963.

Hersov, L. A. "Refusal to Go to School." *Journal of Child Psychology and Psychiatry*, 1960, *1* (1), 137-145.

Hill, J. P. "Some Perspectives on Adolescence in American Society." Position paper prepared for the Office of Child Development, United States Department of Health, Education, and Welfare, 1973.

Hindelang, M. J., and McDermott, M. J. *Criminal Victimization in Urban Schools*. Albany, N.Y.: Criminal Justice Research Center, 1977.

Johnson, J. H. "Life Events as Stressors in Childhood and Adolescence." In B. B. Lahey and A. E. Kazdin (eds.), *Advances in Clinical Child Psychology*. Vol. 5. New York: Plenum, 1982.

Kelly, J. G. "Toward an Ecological Conception of Preventive Interventions." In J. W. Carter, Jr. (ed.), *Research Contributions from Psychology to Community Mental Health*. New York: Behavioral Publications, 1968.

Lerner, R. M. "Adolescent Maturational Changes and Psychosocial Development: A Dynamic Interactional Perspective." *Journal of Youth and Adolescence*, 1985, *14* (4), 355-372.

Levine, M. "Residential Change and School Adjustment." *The Community Mental Health Journal*, 1966, *2* (1), 61-69.

Levine, M., Vesolowski, J. C., and Corbett, F. J. "Pupil Turnover and Academic Performance in an Inner City Elementary School." *Psychology in the Schools*, 1966, *3*, 153-158.

Mason, W. M., Wong, G. Y., and Entwisle, B. "Contextual Analysis Through the

Multilevel Linear Model." In S. Leinhard (ed.), *Sociological Methodology 1983–1984.* San Francisco: Jossey-Bass, 1983.

Midgley, C. "The World of the Early Adolescent." Paper presented as part of a symposium at the American Educational Research Association Annual Meeting, New Orleans, April 1984.

Miller, N. "Peer Relations in Desegregated Schools." In J. L. Epstein and N. Karweit (eds.), *Friends in School: Patterns of Selection and Influence in Secondary Schools.* Orlando, Fla.: Academic Press, 1983.

Moos, R. H. "A Typology of Junior High and High School Classrooms." *American Educational Research Journal,* 1978, *15* (1), 53–66.

Nisbet, J. D., and Entwisle, N. J. *Age of Transfer to Secondary Education.* London: University of London Press, 1966.

Padin, M. A., Lerner, R. M., and Spiro, A., III. "Stability of Body Attitudes and Self-Esteem in Late Adolescents." *Adolescence,* 1981, *16* (62), 371–384.

Peskin, H., and Livson, N. "Pre- and Post-Pubertal Personality and Adult Psychologic Functioning." *Seminars in Psychology,* 1972, *4,* 343–355.

Rosenbaum, J. E. *Making Inequality: The Hidden Curriculum of High School Tracking.* New York: Wiley-Interscience, 1976.

Rubin, H. T. *Juvenile Justice: Policy, Practice, and Law.* Santa Monica, Calif.: Goodyear, 1979.

Rutter, M., and Hersov, L. *Child Psychiatry: Modern Approaches.* Oxford: Blackwell Scientific Publications, 1977.

Schonhaut, C. I. "An Examination of Education Research as it Pertains to the Grade Organization for the Middle Schools." Unpublished Ed.D. dissertation, Columbia University, 1967.

Simmons, R. G., Carlton-Ford, S. L., and Blyth, D. A. "Predicting How a Child Will Cope with the Transition to Junior High School." In R. M. Lerner and T. T. Foch (eds.), *Biological-Psychosocial Interactions in Early Adolescence: A Life-Span Perspective.* Hillsdale, N.J.: Erlbaum, 1987.

Roberta G. Simmons, Ph.D. is professor of sociology and psychiatry at the University of Minnesota. Her research investigates the linkage of social structure and the self-image, particularly in the context of adolescent development, and as related to the impact of high-cost medical technology.

In talking about adolescent development, how will one
respond to the adolescent's questions, or the questions behind
the adolescent's questions: What is true? What is of value?
Who am I now? Where is my home?

Adolescent Development Reconsidered

Carol Gilligan

In an essay, "On the Modern Element in Modern Literature," Trilling
(1967, pp. 164–165) writes of his discomfort in teaching the course in modern literature at Columbia College. No literature, he observes, "has ever
been so shockingly personal as ours—it asks every question that is forbid-
den in polite society. It asks us if we are content with our marriages, with
our family lives, with our professional lives, with our friends. . . . It asks
us if we are content with ourselves, if we are saved or damned." How is
one to teach such literature? After addressing the technicalities of verse
patterns, irony, and prose conventions, the teacher must confront the neces-

The research discussed in this chapter was supported by grants from
Marilyn Brachman Hoffman, the Geraldine Rockefeller Dodge Foundation, the
Rockefeller Foundation, the Joseph S. Klingenstein Foundation, and the Lilly
Foundation. The author is very grateful for the help of Mrs. Hoffman, Scott McVay,
Valerie Peed, Phoebe Cottingham, Joseph Klingenstein, Susan Wisely, the principals
and teachers who joined in this collaboration, and the leaders of the Boys' and
Girls' Clubs of Boston. Special thanks is extended to Bernard Kaplan, Jane Lilien-
feld, Jim Gilligan, and Diana Baumrind for their criticisms and responses to the
research. Thanks is also due to Mary Hartman, dean of Douglass College, and Ferris
Olin as well as the members of the Laurie Chair seminars for a stimulating and
responsive environment in which to work. For the invitations that stimulated both
the writing and rewriting of this chapter, the author is grateful to Robert Blum.

C. E. Irwin, Jr. (ed.). *Adolescent Social Behavior and Health.*
New Directions for Child Development, no. 37. San Francisco: Jossey-Bass, Fall 1987.

sity of bearing personal testimony, "must use whatever authority he may possess to say whether or not a work is true, and if not, why not, and if so, why so." Yet one can do this only at considerable cost to one's privacy. What disturbs Trilling is that in the absence of such confrontation, the classroom lesson exemplifies the very problem displayed in the novels—the costs of detachment and dispassion in the face of what is most intensely passionate and personal.

To talk about health of adolescents raises a similar problem. Once we have covered the technicalities of physical disease and psychic mechanisms, how will we respond to the adolescent's questions, or the questions behind the adolescent's questions: What is true? What is of value? Who am I now? Where is my home? I have studied identity and moral development by listening to the ways in which people speak about themselves and about conflicts and choices they face. In this context, I have thought about the nature of psychological growth as it pertains to questions of truth and of value. Adolescence is a naturally occurring time of transition—a time when changes happen that affect the experience of self and relationships with others. Thus adolescence is a situation for epistemological crisis, an age when issues of interpretation come to the fore. The turbulence and indeterminacy of adolescence, long noted and often attributed to conflicts over sexuality and aggression, can also be traced to these interpretive problems. In this chapter, I will join concerns about the development of contemporary adolescents with concerns about questions of interpretation within psychology. I will begin by specifying four reasons for reconsidering the psychology of adolescence at this time and then offer a new framework for thinking about adolescent development and secondary education.

Four Reasons for Reconsidering Adolescent Development

First, the view of childhood has changed. Since adolescence denotes the transition from childhood to adulthood, what constitutes development in adolescence hinges on how one views the childhood that precedes it and the adulthood that follows. Recent research on infancy and early childhood reveals the young child to be far more social than psychologists previously imagined, calling into question most descriptions of the beginnings or early stages of cognitive, social, and moral development. Stern's recent book, *The Interpersonal World of the Infant* (1985) and Kagan's *The Nature of the Child* (1984) document the interpersonal capabilities and the social nature of young children: their responsiveness to others and their appreciation of standards. Previously described as "locked up in egocentrism," as "fused" with others, as capable only of "parallel play," the young child now is observed to initiate and sustain connection with others, to engage in patterns of social interaction with others and thus to create relationships with them. Emde, Johnson, and Easterbrooks's (1987) research shows that nine-month-old babies prefer mothers to respond to their actions rather than to mimic, or mirror, their behavior. In addition, infants by this age have established distinctive patterns of social interaction with others, so that their relationships can be differentiated in these terms by the researcher, and presumably by the baby, since the patterns repeat. Thus relationships, or connections with others, are known to the young child as patterns of interaction that occur in time and that extend through time: themes and variations.

It may well be that the tension between this felt knowledge of human connection, this earliest grasp of what relationship means, and the ability to represent this knowledge in language underlies many psychological problems people experience and also many problems within the field of psychology itself. Despite the fact that psychologists constantly talk about interaction or relationship—between self and others, between person and environment—the language of psychology is filled with static, visual images of separation. Thus psychologists delineate borders and boundaries in an effort to classify and categorize and ultimately to predict and control human behavior, whereas behavior, especially when observed in its natural settings, often resists such classification. At present, Hoffman's (1976) observations of empathy and altruism in young children and Gottman's (1983) monograph "How Children Become Friends"—studies that derive from watching children in the natural settings of their daily lives—challenge existing stage theories of social and moral development by revealing the disparity between the stage theory description of the young child as asocial or amoral and the intensely social and also moral nature of the young child's relationships with others. Like Bowlby (1973, 1980), who observed the young child to grieve the loss that separation entails, Hoffman saw young children perceive and respond to the needs of others, and Gottman saw children remember their friends—even after surprisingly long intervals of physical distance and time.

These radical changes in the view of childhood necessitate a revision in the description of adolescent development, since they alter the foundation on which psychologists have premised development in the teenage years. If social responsiveness and moral concern are normally present in early childhood, their absence in adolescence becomes surprising. Rather than asking why such capacities have failed to emerge by adolescence, implying that the child is stuck at some earlier or lower stage, one would ask instead what has happened to the responsiveness of infancy, how have the child's capacities for relationship been diminished or lost? This change in perspective also offers a new way of thinking about resistance—especially the signs of resistance often noted among teenage girls (Gilligan, 1986a). Rather than signaling conflicts over separation, such resistance may reflect girls' perception that connections with others are endangered for girls in the teenage years on a variety of levels.

The second reason for reconsidering what is meant by development in adolescence follows directly from this observation. Repeatedly, the inattention to girls has been noted as a lacuna in the literature on adolescence (Bettelheim, 1961; Adelson and Doehrman, 1980)—which raises the question: What has been missed by not studying girls? The answer generally is felt to be something about relationships, and those who have studied girls and women confirm this speculation. Konopka (1966, p. 40), who entered the locked world of delinquent girls to learn about their own stories, found that these stories were centrally about "loneliness accompanied by despair"—a desperation of loneliness "based on a feeling of being unprotected, being incapable of making and finding friends, being surrounded by an anonymous and powerful adult world." Konopka observed that although the need for connection with others, which means involvement with others who are "real friends" or with an adult who appears as "a person," is unusually intense among delinquent girls, the "need for *dependence* . . . seems to exist in all adolescent girls." Miller (1976), writing about women who come for psychotherapy, noted that women's sense of self is built around being able to make and then maintain connections with others and that the loss of relationships is experienced by many women as tantamount to a loss of self. Listening to girls and women speaking about themselves and about their experiences of conflict and choice, I heard conceptions of self and morality that implied a different way of thinking about relationships—one that often had set women apart from the mainstream of Western thought because of its central premise that self and others were connected and interdependent.

Thus to say what is true—that girls and women have not been much studied is only to begin to appreciate what such study might entail. To reconsider adolescent development in light of the inattention to girls and women is to hold in abeyance the meaning of such key terms of psychological analysis as *self* and *development* and perhaps above all *relationship*.

For the present, to take seriously psychologists' past omission of girls and women and to see this absence as potentially significant means to suspend for the moment all discussion of sex differences until the standards of assessment and the terms of comparison can be drawn from studies of girls and women as well as boys and men. The deep sense of outrage and despair over disconnection, tapped by Konopka, Miller, myself, and others—the strong feelings and judgments often made by girls and women about excluding, leaving out, and abandoning, as well as the desperate actions girls and women often take in the face of detachment or indifference or lack of concern—may reflect an awareness on some level of the disjunction between women's lives and Western culture. Yet the equally strong feelings often expressed by girls and women that such feelings are illegitimate and the judgments often made that such exclusion is justified or deserved serve to undercut this awareness. What Adelson and Doehrman

(1980, p. 114) call "the inattention to girls, and the processes of feminine development in adolescence" tacitly supports the suspicion of girls and women that nothing of importance or value can be learned by studying them. In the moral conflicts adolescent girls and women describe, a central and searing dilemma is about this problem of disconnection: Is it better, women ask, to turn away from others or to abandon themselves. This question—whether to be selfish or selfless in choosing between self and others rests on the premise that genuine connection must fail. One reason for reconsidering the psychology of adolescence is to examine this premise.

The third reason for reconsideration pertains specifically to cognitive development and involves the definition of cognition—what knowing and also thinking mean. Following Sputnik in the late 1950s, Americans became concerned about the state of math and science education as part of an effort to "catch up with the Russians." The revival of Piaget's work in the early 1960s provided a psychological rationale for this endeavor, since in Piaget's view cognitive development was identical to the growth of mathematical and scientific thinking (see for example Inhelder and Piaget, 1958). This conception of cognitive development conveys a view of the individual as living in a timeless world of abstract rules. Within this framework, there is no rationale for teaching history or languages or writing or for paying attention to art and music. In fact, the flourishing of Piagetian theory within psychology over the past two decades has coincided with the decline of all these subjects in the school curriculum.

Educators looking to psychology to justify curriculum decisions still can find little basis for teaching history or for encouraging students to learn more than one language or for emphasizing complex problems of interpretation and the strategies needed for reading ambiguous texts. In the timeless world of critical thinking, the fact that one cannot say exactly the same thing in French and in English becomes in essence irrelevant to the development of intelligence. Ravitch (1985) recently has chronicled the decline of historical knowledge among high school students and lamented the transposition of history into social science. Yet the humanities, in order to gain funding or to defend their place within the curriculum, have often had to justify their educational value in terms psychologists have derived from analyzing the structure of mathematical and scientific reasoning.

The ahistorical approach to human events underlies the fourth reason for reconsideration: namely, the overriding value psychologists have placed on separation, individuation, and autonomy. To see self-sufficiency as the hallmark of maturity conveys a view of adult life that is at odds with the human condition—a view that cannot sustain the kinds of long-term commitments and involvements with others that are necessary for raising and educating a child or for citizenship in a democratic society (see Arendt, 1958). The equation of development with separation and of maturity with independence presumes a radical discontinuity of generations and encourages a vision of human experience that is essentially divorced from history or time. The tendency for psychologists to characterize adolescence as the time of second individuation (Blos, 1967) and to celebrate an identity that is self-wrought (Erikson, 1958) encourages a way of speaking in which the interdependence of human life and the reliance of people on one another becomes largely unrepresented or tacit. The way in which this value framework colors the interpretation of research findings is exemplified by an article recently published by Pipp and others (1985), who set out to discover how adolescents view their relationships with their parents over time—what changes they see in such connections from early childhood to late adolescence. Thus college sophomores were asked through drawings and questionnaire ratings to indicate the nature of their relationship with their parents at five points in time ranging from early childhood to the present. The authors note two distinct trends. One was expected and is familiar to anyone conversant with developmental theory: a linear progression whereby incrementally over time child and parent move from a relationship of inequality toward an ideal of equality. Thus the child is portrayed as gaining steadily in responsibility, dominance, and independence in relation to the parents, who correspondingly decline on all these dimensions. With this shift in the balance of power, child and parent become increasingly alike or similar over time. The other trend was unanticipated and showed a striking discontinuity. With respect to variables pertaining to love and closeness, college sophomores saw their relationships with their parents as closer at present than in the years preceding, more similar in this respect to their relationships with their parents in early childhood. In addition, differences emerged along these two dimensions between the ways students represented their relationships with their mothers and fathers in that they felt more responsibility toward their mothers, whom they perceived as especially friendly, and they felt more similar to their fathers, whom they perceived as more dominant.

The unexpected finding of two asymmetrical lines of development tied to different dimensions of relationship is of great interest to me because it corroborates the developmental model I have derived from analyzing the ways people describe themselves and make moral judgments—a model built on the distinction between equality and attachment as two dimensions of relationship that shape the experience of self and define the terms of moral conflict. For the moment, however, I wish to focus on the way Pipp and others interpret their findings, specifically to note that in discussing their results, they collapse the two trends they have discovered and in doing so reveal an overriding concern with equality and independence. The fact that nineteen-year-olds describe themselves as their parents' children thus is taken by Pipp and others (1985, p. 1001) as a sign of limitation, an indication that the process of individuation is not yet complete.

Although [our subjects] felt themselves to be more independent of the relationship than their parents were, there were
indications that they still felt themselves to be their parents'
children. . . . The results suggest that the individuation process is still ongoing at the age of 19. It would be interesting
to see whether it continues throughout adulthood.

With this interpretation, the authors align themselves with the field of
psychology in general. Viewing childhood attachments as a means to separation, they portray continuing connections between adolescents and parents as a sign of dependence, negatively valued and considered as a source
of limitation.

To summarize this first section, the need to reconsider adolescent
development at present stems from changes in the understanding of
infancy and childhood, from the recognition that girls have not been much
studied and that studies of girls are overlooked or not cited, from the observation that Piagetian theories of cognitive development provide no rationale for roughly half of what has traditionally been regarded as the essence
of a liberal arts or humanistic education, and from the fact that a psychology of adolescence, anchored in the values of separation and independence,
fails to represent the interdependence of adult life and thus conveys a
distorted image of the human condition, an image that fosters what is
currently called the culture of narcissism.

I take from these observations several cautions: that there is a need
for new concepts and new categories of interpretation; that the accumula-
tion of data according to old conceptual frameworks simply extends these
problems; that the assessment of sex differences cannot be undertaken until
female development is better understood; that such understanding may
change the description of both male and female development; and that the
approach to the psychology of adolescence and to subjects pertaining to
adolescent development and education must be informed by the insights
of such disciplines as anthropology, history, and literature. Specifically,
psychologists need to incorporate anthropologists' recognition of the
dangers in imposing one set of ethnocentric categories on a different population and to take on the concerns of anthropologists, historians, and
literary critics with the complexity of interpretation and the construction
of alternative world views.

Formulating an Approach

In the 1971 issue of *Daedalus* devoted to the subject of early adolescence, several articles addressed the question of values. If the high school
does not have a coherent set of values or a moral philosophy, Kagan
argued (as did Kohlberg and myself), it cannot engage the commitment of

its students. The school and the culture at large must offer some justification for learning to adolescents who are distracted by other concerns, who are capable of spotting contradiction, who have a keen eye for adult hypocrisy, and who are unwilling to put their self-esteem on the line when failure seems inescapable. Bettelheim (1965, p. 106) linked the problems of youth to the problem of generations: "Whenever the older generation has lost its bearings, the younger generation is lost with it. The positive alternatives of emulation or revolt are replaced with the lost quality of neither." Erikson (1975, p. 223), writing at a time when the dissent of contemporary youth was rising, noted that for adults "to share true authority with the young would mean to acknowledge something which adults have learned to mistrust in themselves: a truly ethical potential." To Erikson, ethical concerns were a natural meeting ground between adults and adolescents, both rendered uncertain by the predicament of modern civilization.

Yet if ethical questions are inescapable in relations between adults and adolescents, if the problems of adolescents are in some sense a barometer of the health of civilization, a measure of the culture's productive and reproductive potential, the issues raised by Trilling become central: How are adults to address the ethical problems of modern society? What claims to moral authority do the teachers of adolescents possess? The great modern novels that Trilling was teaching had as a central and controlling theme "the disenchantment of our culture with culture itself . . . a bitter line of hostility to civilization" (1967, p. 60). Thus the urgency of the questions: Are we content with our marriages, our work, and ourselves? How do we envision salvation? What wisdom can we pass on to the next generation? Twentieth-century history has only heightened ambivalence toward the life of civilization by demonstrating in one of the most highly educated and cultured of nations a capacity for moral atrocity so extreme as to strain the meaning of words. In light of this history, any equation of morality with culture or intelligence or education is immediately suspect, and this suspicion has opened the way for the current revival of religious fundamentalism and of terrorism, as well as for the present skepticism about nineteenth-century ideas about development or progress. The idea of "surrendering oneself to experience without regard to self-interest or conventional morality, of escaping wholly from the societal bonds, is," Trilling (1967, p. 82) notes, "an 'element' somewhere in the mind of every modern person." This element is manifest in one form or another in many of the problems of today's adolescents.

The awesome power of the irrational in human behavior is the subject of both classical tragedy and modern psychology, each attempting in different ways to untangle and explain its logic, to understand why people pursue paths that are clearly marked as self-destructive—why, for example, teenagers stop eating, take drugs, commit suicide, and in a variety of other ways wreak havoc with their future. Two approaches currently characterize the response of professionals to these signs of disease. One relies on the imposition of control, the effort to override a tortuous reason with behavior modification and biofeedback, to focus attention simply on physical survival by teaching skills for managing stress and regulating food and alcohol consumption. The other approach reaches into reason and joins the humanistic faith in the power of education with the insights of modern psychology. Positing human development as the aim of education, it turns attention to the question: What constitutes and fosters development?

My interest in adolescence is anchored in the second approach. It was spurred by Erikson's attention to the relationship between life history and history and by two insights in the work of Kohlberg: First, that following the Nazi holocaust, psychologists must address the question of moral relativism, and second, that adolescents are passionately interested in moral questions. Thus adolescence may be a crucial time for moral education. Erikson's study of Luther highlighted the central tie between questions of identity and questions of morality in the adolescent years. But it also called attention to a set of beliefs that extend from the theology of Luther's Reformation into the ideology of contemporary psychology: a world view in which the individual is embarked on a solitary journey toward personal salvation, a world view that is centered on the values of autonomy and independence. Luther's statements of repudiation and affirmation, "I am not" and "Here I stand" have become emblematic of the identity crisis in modern times—a crisis that begins with the separation of self from childhood identifications and attachments and ends with some version of Luther's statement: "I have faith, therefore I am justified." In a secular age, the faith and the justification have become psychological. The limitations of this vision have been elaborated by a variety of social critics and are closely connected to the reasons I have given for reconsidering the psychology of adolescence: the view of childhood attachments as dispensable or replaceable, the absence of women from the cosmology, the equation of thinking with formal logic, and the value placed of self-sufficiency and independence. Such criticisms are augmented by the facts of recent social history: the rise in teenage suicides, eating disorders, and educational problems. The need at present for new directions in theory and practice seem clear.

Two Moral Voices: Two Frameworks for Problem Solving

My approach to development is attentive to a moral voice that reveals the lineaments of an alternative world view and is grounded in seemingly anomalous data from studies involving girls and women (Gilligan, 1977, 1982, 1986b)—moral judgments that did not fit the definition of moral and self-descriptions at odds with the concept of self. The data that initially appeared discrepant became the basis for a reformulation, grounds for thinking again about what self, morality, and relationship mean.

Two moral voices that signal different ways of thinking about what constitutes a moral problem and how such problems can be addressed or resolved draw attention to the fact that a story can be told from different angles and a situation seen in different lights. Like ambiguous figure perception where the same picture can be seen as a vase or two faces, the basic elements of moral judgment—self, others, and relationship—can be organized in different ways, depending on how relationship is imagined or construed. From the perspective of someone seeking or loving justice, relationships are organized in terms of equality, symbolized by the balancing of scales. Moral concerns focus on problems of inequality or oppression, and the moral ideal is one of reciprocity, or equal respect. From the perspective of someone seeking or valuing care, relationship connotes responsiveness, or attachment, a resiliency of connection that is symbolized by a network, or web. Moral concerns focus on problems of detachment or disconnection or abandonment, and the moral ideal is one of attention and response. Since equality and attachment are dimensions that characterize all forms of human connection, all relationships can be seen in both ways and spoken of in both sets of terms. Yet by adopting one or another moral voice or standpoint, people can highlight problems that are associated with different kinds of vulnerability and focus attention on different types of concern.

Evidence that justice and care concerns can be distinguished in people's narratives about moral conflict and choice and that these concerns organize people's thinking about decisions they make comes from a series of studies in which people were asked to discuss conflicts and choices that they faced. In essence, by asking people to speak about times when they confronted dilemmas, it was possible to examine how people think about the age-old questions of how to live and what to do. Most of the people who participated in these studies, primarily North American adolescents and adults, raised considerations of both justice and care when describing an experience of moral conflict. Yet they also tended to focus their attention on one set of concerns and minimally represent the other. The surprising finding of these studies was the extent of this "focus" phenomenon. For example, in a study (Gilligan and Attanucci, 1985) where focus was defined as 75 percent or more considerations pertaining either to issues of justice or to issues of care, fifty-three out of eighty educationally advantaged adolescents and adults, or two-thirds of the sample, demonstrated focus. The remaining third raised roughly equal numbers of justice and care considerations.

The tendency for people to organize experiences of conflict and choice largely in terms of justice or in terms of care has been a constant finding of the research on moral orientation, ranging from Lyons's (1983) and Langdale's (1983) reports of orientation predominance, to the more stringent analysis of orientation focus by Gilligan and Attanucci (1985), to the most recent analysis of narrative strategies (Brown and others, 1987). This takes into account not simply the number or proportion of justice and care considerations raised but also the way in which concerns about justice and care are presented in relation to one another and in relation to the speaker or narrator of the dilemma—whether justice and care are presented as separate concerns or integrated, whether one or both sets of concerns are aligned with the narrator or claimed as the speaker's own terms. The fact that two moral voices can repeatedly be distinguished in narratives of moral conflict and choice and the fact that people tend to focus their attention either on problems of unfairness or problems of disconnection gives credence to the interpretation of justice and care as frameworks that organize moral thinking and feelings. The focus phenomenon, however, suggests that people tend to lose sight of one perspective or to silence one set of concerns in arriving at decisions or in justifying choices they have made.

The tendency to focus was equally characteristic of the men and the women studied, suggesting that loss of perspective is a liability that both sexes share. There were striking sex differences, however, in the direction of focus. Of the thirty-one men who demonstrated focus, thirty focused on justice; of the twenty-two women who demonstrated focus, ten focused on justice and twelve on care. Care focus, although not characteristic of all women, was almost exclusively a female phenomenon in Brown and others' study of educationally advantaged North Americans. If girls and women were eliminated from the study, care focus in moral reasoning would virtually disappear.

With this clarification of the different voice phenomenon—the thematic shift in outlook or perspective, the change in the terms of moral discourse and self description, and the empirical association with women—it becomes possible to turn to new questions about development in adolescence and psychological interpretation, as well as to concerns about moral relativism and moral education. It is noteworthy that both sexes raise considerations of care in describing moral conflicts they face and thus identify problems of care and connection as subjects of moral concern. Yet it is women's elaboration of care considerations that reveals the coherence of a care ethic as a framework for decision—its premises as a world view or way of constructing social reality, its logic as a problem-solving strategy, and its significance as a focal point for evaluating actions and thinking about choice. The description of care concerns as the focus of a coherent moral perspective rather than as a sign of deficiency in women's moral reasoning or a subordinate set of concerns within a justice framework (such as special obligations or personal dilemmas) recasts the moral domain as one comprising at least two moral orientations. Moral maturity presumably would entail an ability to see in both ways and to speak both languages, and the relationship between these two moral perspectives or voices becomes a key question for investigation.

The significance of the concept of moral orientation for thinking about development in adolescence is illuminated by a brilliant study designed and conducted by Johnston (1985). Johnston set out to examine Polanyi's (1958) suggestion that there are two conflicting aspects of formalized intelligence; one that depends on the acquisition of formalized instruments (such as propositional logic) and one that depends on the "pervasive participation of the knowing person in the act of knowing." Polanyi (1958, p. 70) considers this latter kind of intelligence to rest on "an art which is essentially inarticulate." Johnston's question was whether this way of knowing could be articulated. Her approach to this question was informed by Vygotsky's (1978, p. 57) theory that all of the higher cognitive functions (voluntary attention, logical memory, formation of concepts) originate as actual relations between individuals, so that in the course of development "an interpersonal process is transformed into an intrapersonal one." This is a theory that allows for individual differences and that can explain how different experiences of relationships might lead to different ways of thinking about a problem—such as the sex differences in early childhood relationships that Chodorow (1978) has described. Furthermore, groups like women whose experience in general has been neglected in considering the sources of cognitive and moral proficiency may exemplify ways of knowing or thinking that appear, in the present context, to be inarticulate. Johnston's question was whether tacit knowledge, or intuitive forms of knowing—what Belenky and others (1986) have subsequently called connected knowing—might appear as different forms of moral problem solving.

Thus Johnston asked sixty eleven- and fifteen-year-olds from two schools in a typical middle-class suburb to state and to solve the problem posed in two of Aesop's fables. Of the sixty children, fifty-four (or fifty-six, depending on the fable) initially cast the problem either as a problem of rights or as a problem of response, framing it either as a conflict of claims that could be resolved by appealing to a fair procedure or a rule for adjudicating disputes or as a problem of need, which raised the question of whether or how it was possible to respond to all of the needs. Each way of defining the problem was associated with a different problem-solving strategy, thus tying moral orientation to the development of different kinds of reasoning. For example, in the fable, "The Moles and the Porcupine" (see Exhibit 1), a justice strategy focused on identifying and prioritizing conflicting rights or claims. ("The porcupine has to go definitely. It's the moles' house.") In contrast, a care strategy focused on identifying needs and creating a solution responsive to all of the needs. ("Cover the porcuping with a blanket [so that the moles will not be stuck and the porcupine will have shelter]" or "Dig a bigger hole.") It is important to stress that these two approaches are not opposites or mirror images of one another (with justice uncaring and care unjust). Instead, they constitute different ways of organizing the problem that lead to different reasoning strategies—different ways of thinking about what is happening and what to do.

Exhibit 1. The Porcupine and the Moles

It was growing cold, and a porcupine was looking for a home. He found a most desirable cave, but saw it was occupied by a family of moles.

"Would you mind if I shared your home for the winter?" the porcupine asked the moles.

The generous moles consented, and the porcupine moved in. But the cave was small, and every time the moles moved around, they were scratched by the porcupine's sharp quills. The moles endured this discomfort as long as they could. Then at last they gathered courage to approach their visitor. "Pray leave," they said, "and let us have our cave to ourselves once again."

"Oh no!" said the porcupine. "This place suits me very well."

The brilliance of Johnston's design lay in the fact that after the children had stated and solved the fable problem, she asked, "Is there another way to think about this problem?" About half of the children, somewhat more fifteen- than eleven-year-olds, spontaneously switched orientation and solved the problem in the other mode. Others did so following a cue as to the form such a switch might take. ("Some people say you could have a rule; some people say you could solve the dilemma so that all of the animals will be satisfied.") Then Johnston asked, "Which of these solutions is the better solution?" With few exceptions, the children answered this question, saying which solution was better and explaining why it was preferable.

This study is a watershed about developmental theory and research practices. The fact that people solve a problem in one way clearly does not mean that they do not have access to other approaches. Furthermore, a person's initial or spontaneous approach to a problem is not necessarily the one he or she deems preferable. Eleven- and fifteen-year-olds are able to explain why they adopt problem-solving strategies that they see as problematic, to give reasons for why they put aside ways of thinking that in their own eyes seem preferable. Whether there are reasons other than the ones they cite is, in this context, beside the point. The fact that boys who choose justice strategies but say they prefer care solutions but consider care solutions to be naive and unworkable is, in itself, of significance. For example, in one high school, students of both sexes tended to characterize care-focused solutions or inclusive problem-solving strategies as utopian or outdated; one student linked them with impractical Sunday school teachings, one with the outworn philosophy of hippies. Presumably, students in the school who voiced care strategies would encounter these characterizations.

The tendency for children to define the fable problem in terms either of rights or of response, combined with their ability to switch orientations, heightens the analogy to ambiguous figure perception but also raises the question: Why do some people focus on justice and some on care when considering the same problem? Furthermore, why do some people see rights solutions as better and others see response solutions as preferable in the same situation? Johnston found sex differences in both spontaneous moral orientation and preferred orientation, with boys more often choosing and preferring justice formulations and girls more often choosing and preferring care strategies. In addition, she found fable differences, indicating that moral orientation is associated both with the sex of the reasoner and with the problem being considered. (See Langdale, 1983, for similar findings.)

Since people can adopt at least two moral standpoints and can solve problems in at least two different ways, the choice of moral standpoint, whether implicit or explicit, becomes an important feature of moral decision making and of research on moral development. The choice of moral standpoint adds a new dimension to the role commonly accorded the self in moral decision making. Traditionally, the self is described as choosing whether or not to enact moral standards or principles, as having or not having a good will. Yet the self, whether conceived as a narrator of moral conflict or as a protagonist in a moral drama, also chooses, consciously or unconsciously, where to stand—what signs to look for and what voices to listen to in thinking about what is happening (what is the problem) and what to do. People may have a preferred way of seeing and may be attuned to different voices, so that one voice or another is more readily heard or understood. Johnston demonstrated that at least by age 11, children know and can explain the logic of two problem-solving strategies and will indicate why they see one or the other as preferable. In adolescence, when thinking becomes more reflective and more self-conscious, moral orientation may become closely entwined with self-definition, so that the sense of self or feelings of personal integrity become aligned with a particular way of seeing or speaking.

But adolescence, the time when thinking becomes self-consciously interpretive, is also the time when the interpretive schemes of the culture, including the system of social norms, values, and roles, impinge more directly on perception and judgment, defining within the framework of a given society what is the "right way" to see and to feel and to think—the way "we" think. Thus adolescence is the age when thinking becomes conventional. Moral standpoint, a feature of an individual's moral reasoning, is also a characteristic of interpretive schemes, including the conventions of interpretation or the intellectual conventions that are taught in secondary education. The justice focus, which is explicit in most theories of moral development (see Freud, [1925] 1961; Piaget, [1932] 1965; Kohlberg, 1969), also characterizes and makes plain the correlation found between tests of moral development and tests of cognitive and social and emotional development; although measuring different things, all these tests may be measuring from the same angle. Thus a care focus that otherwise can be viewed as one aspect of moral reasoning becomes a crucial perspective on an interpretive level, challenging the prevailing world view. Here the questions raised by Trilling become especially pertinent, articulating a central theme in modern culture that is at odds with the dominant viewpoint in contemporary psychology—the theme of disenchantment. Psychology's response to the moral crisis of modern civilization has become a kind of heady optimism, reflected in the language of current stage theories and intervention promises, conveying the impression that the nature of moral maturity is clear and the road to development apparent. To bring in a standpoint missing from such theories enlarges the definition of cognition and morality and renders the portrayal of human development and moral dilemmas more complex. The following example, taken from a study of high school students, speaks directly to these questions and suggests how a prevailing justice orientation may impinge on the judgments adolescents make, influencing both the concerns that they voice and also what they hold back or keep silent. The example contains both a theoretical point and a methodological caution: Two judgments, one directly stated and one indirectly presented, highlight a developmental tension between detachment and connection and underscore the limitations of data gathered without attention to the issue of standpoint or the possibility of alternative frameworks or world views. At the heart of this illustration of alternative world views and the problems posed by alternative world views is a critical but subtle shift in perspective, caught colloquially by the difference between being centered in oneself and being self-centered.

An Example of Alternative World Views

A high school student, Anne, was attending a traditional preparatory school for academically talented and ambitious students, a boy's school that in recent years became coeducational. When asked to describe a moral conflict she faced, Anne spoke about her decision not to buy cigarettes for someone who asked her to do so. Her reasoning focused on considerations of justice: "If I am against smoking, but yet I buy cigarettes for a person, I think I am contradicting myself." Noncontradiction here means reciprocity in the sense of applying the same standard to herself and to others, treating others as she would treat herself or want to be treated by them, and thereby showing equal respect for persons. Asked if she thought she had done the right thing, she answers, "Yes . . . I think it was, because I did not contradict myself, because I held with what I believed." Thus she assesses the rightness of her decision by examining the consistency between her actions and her beliefs, justified on grounds of respect for life and valuing health. Then she is asked, "Is there another way to see the problem?" and she says,

> Well, no. I mean yes. It is not as simple as buying cigarettes or not. It has a lot to do with everything that I believe in. . . . In another sense, it represents how I deal with what I believe. I try not to break down just because somebody pressures me, but I don't feel like I get into situations like they always write about in books. . . . I don't think people are represented the way they are sometimes.

It is important to emphasize that this intimation of another way of seeing, and the suggestion that the way people and situations are commonly represented may not be an accurate representation, occurs only after the interpretive question "Is there another way to see the problem?" is raised. And the interpretive question leads to confusion, to a dense statement that appears to alternate between two perspectives, one elaborated and one implied. The implied perspective, which "has a lot to do with everything that I believe in," is only clarified when Anne speaks about a friend whom she characterizes as "self-centered." In this context, the meaning of being self-centered shifts from "holding with what I believe" to "not thinking about how one's words or actions affect other people." With this shift, the alternative world view and the problem posed by alternative world views become clear.

Anne says that her friend does not recognize how what she says affects other people: "She does not think about how it affects them, but just about the fact that she told them." In other words, she acts as if speaking could be divorced from listening, or words from interpretation. Because her friend is inattentive to differences in interpretation, she "does not always recognize that what she likes to hear is not what other people like to hear, but may hurt their feelings." She is self-centered in that she does not realize that "other people are not all like her."

Thus attention to differences in interpretation is central to making connection with others. The interpretive question raised by the researcher that leads Anne to attend to the issue of perspective also leads her into a way of thinking where the failure to see differences becomes morally problematic, signifying carelessness or detachment (being self-centered) and creating the conditions for the unwitting infliction of hurt. This is a very different set of concerns from the concerns about noncontradiction and acting consistently with her beliefs, which characterized Anne's justice reasoning. With the shift in perspective, the word *autonomy* takes on different connotations: To be self-regulating or self-governing can mean being centered in oneself but it also can mean not attending or responding to others. The tension between these two ways of seeing and listening creates a conflict that, as Anne says, is "not as simple as buying cigarettes or not," a conflict that in addition is not well represented by the common depiction of adolescent moral conflicts as peer-pressure problems.

Asked if she had learned anything from the experience, Anne speaks in two voices. She asserts her satisfaction with her ability "to stay with what I believe, and as far as learning something from it, I was able to say no and so I could say it again." But she also asserts her unease about shutting herself off from others, about becoming impervious to the changing circumstances of her life and unresponsive to the people around her.

> But I don't know that I will always say no to everything. You can't all the time, and as you make better friends and as you are under different circumstances and different situations, I think my answers will change—as I become more like the people in this school. Because no matter where you are, you tend to become at least a little like the people around you.

Anne does not doubt the wisdom or the rightness of her decision to say no in this instance, but the incident raises a further question: How can she stay with herself and also be with other people? Viewing life as lived in the changing medium of time and seeing herself as open to the people around her, she believes that in time both she and her answers will change. The dilemma or tension she faces is not that of peer pressure— how to say no to her friends or classmates. Instead, it stems from a different way of thinking about herself in relation to others, a way that leads into the question of what relationship, or in this instance friendship, means.

The ability to sustain two perspectives that offer divergent views of a scene or to tell a story from two different angles can be taken as a marker of cognitive and moral growth in the adolescent years—a sign perhaps in the context of ordinary living of what Keats called "negative capability," the ability of the artist to enter into and to take on ways of seeing and speaking that differ from one's own. For example, with respect to the question of separation or individuation as it pertains to adolescents' perceptions of their relationships with their parents, one teenager says, "I am not only my mother's daughter, I am also Susan." Another, describing her anger at her holding-on mother, recalls herself as saying to her mother, "You will always be my mother. . . . I will always be your daughter, but you have to let go." These not only/but also constructions used by teenage girls in describing themselves in relation to their mothers convey a view of change as occurring in the context of continuing attachment and imply a vision of development that does not entail detachment or carry the implication that relationships can be replaced. From this standpoint, the moral problems engendered by the transformations of relationships in adolescence pertain not only to injustice and oppression but also to abandonment and disloyalty. Thus seen, development in adolescence takes on new dimensions. The much discussed problem of moral relativism is joined by the problem of moral reductionism, the temptation to simplify human dilemmas by claiming that there is only one moral standpoint.

A study conducted at a high school for girls clarified the ways in which moral conflicts in adolescence catch the transformation of relationships along the two dimensions of equality and attachment, highlighting problems of unfairness but also problems of disconnection. As the balance of power between child and adult shifts with the child's coming of age, so too the experience and the meaning of connection change. What constitutes attachment in early childhood does not constitute connection in adolescence, given the sexual changes of puberty and also the growth of subjective and reflective thought. Thus the question arises: What are the analogues in adolescence to the responsive engagement that psychologists now find so striking in infancy and early childhood? What constitutes genuine connection in the adolescent years?

I raise this question to explicate a point of view that at first glance may seem inconsequential or even antithetical to concerns about adolescent development and health. One can readily applaud Anne's decision not to buy cigarettes for another (argued in terms of justice) and see her ability to say no as one that will stand her in good stead. My intention is not to qualify this judgment or to diminish the importance of this ability but to stress the importance of another as well. Like concerns about submitting or yielding to pressure from others, concerns about not listening or becoming cut off from others are also vital concerns. The ability to create and sustain human connection may hinge in adolescence on the ability to differentiate true from false relationship—to read the signs that distinguish authentic from inauthentic forms of connection and thus to protect the wish for relationship or the openness to others from overwhelming disappointment or defeat. The capacity for detachment in adolescence, heightened by the growth of formal operational thinking and generally prized as the hallmark of cognitive and moral development, is thus doubled edged, signaling an ability to think critically about thinking but also a potential for becoming, in Anne's terms, self-centered. Although detachment connotes the dispassion that signifies fairness in justice reasoning, the ability to stand back from oneself and from others and to weigh conflicting claims evenhandedly in the abstract, detachment also connotes the absence of connection and creates the conditions for carelessness or violation, for violence toward others or oneself.

The adolescent's question "Where am I going?" is rendered problematic because adolescents lack experience in the ways of adult work and love. High school students, including inner-city youth living in poverty, often speak about their plans to work and have a family. Yet even if such goals are clearly envisioned, teenagers have no experience of how to reach them. When you do not know where you are going or how the route goes, the range of interpretation opens up enormously. The adolescent's question "Where is my home" is commonly raised for college students who wonder, is it here at school, or back in Ohio, or in Larchmont? Where will it be in the future? How do I interpret whatever new moves I make in my life?

These interpretive questions fall on the line of intellectual and ethical development that Perry (1970) traced—a line leading from the belief that truth is objective and known by authorities to the realization that all truth is contextually relative and responsibility for commitment inescapable. Yet Perry, although addressing the existential dilemma, leaves open the issue of detachment that bothered Trilling, posing the teaching quandary Trilling raised: What commitments can one defend as worth making and on what basis can one claim authority? Erikson (1958) wrote about the penchant of adolescents for absolute truths and totalistic solutions, the proclivity to end, once and for all, all uncertainty and confusion by seizing control and attempting to stop time or blot out, or eliminate, in one way or another the source of confusion—in others or in oneself. Many destructive actions on the part of adolescents can be understood in these terms. Because adolescents are capable not only of abstract logical thinking but also of participating in the act of knowing; because they are in some sense aware of subjectivity and perspective, or point of view; because they are therefore able to see through false claims to authority at the same time as they yearn for right answers or for someone who will tell them how they should live and what they should do; the temptation for adults dealing with adolescents is to opt for the alternatives or permissiveness or authoritarianism and to evade the problems that lie in taking what Baumrind (1978) has called an authoritative stance.

Resisting Detachment

One problem in taking an authoritative stance with adolescents is that many of the adults involved with adolescents have little authority in this society. Therefore, although they may in fact know much about teenagers' lives, they may have little confidence in their knowledge. Rather than claiming authority, they may detach their actions from their judgment and attribute their decisions to the judgments of those who are in positions of greater social power. But another problem lies in the perennial quandary about adolescents: what actions to take in attempting to guide teenagers away from paths clearly marked as destructive and how to read the signs that point in the direction of health. To reconsider the nature of development in adolescence itself raises a question of perspective: From what angle or in what terms shall this reconsideration take place?

Recent studies of adolescents in families and schools have been discovering the obvious, although the need for such diversity also seems obvious since the implications are repeatedly ignored. The studies find that adolescents fare better in situations where adults listen and that mothers and teachers are centrally important in teenagers' lives. Mothers are the parent with whom adolescents typically have the most contact, the one they talk with the most and perceive as knowing most about their lives (Youniss and Smollar, 1985). Most researchers consider it desirable for fathers to be more involved with adolescents, but they find, in general, that fathers do not spend as much time or talk as personally with their teenage children. In studies of schools, teachers are cited as central to the success of secondary education. The good high schools identified by Rutter and others (1979) and by Lightfoot (1983) are characterized by the presence of teachers who are able, within the framework of a coherent set of values or school ethos, to assume authority and to take responsibility for what they do. Yet mothers of adolescents are increasingly single parents living in poverty, and teachers at present are generally unsupported and devalued. Psychological development in adolescence may well hinge on the adolescent's belief that her or his psyche is worth developing, and this belief in turn may hinge on the presence in a teenager's life of an adult who knows and cares about the teenager's psyche. Economic and psychological support for the mothers and the teachers who at present are the primary adults engaged with teenagers may be essential to the success of efforts to promote adolescent development.

The question of what stance or aim or direction to take is focused by the research on moral orientation, which points to two lines of development and to their possible tension. If a focus on care currently provides a critical interpretive standpoint and highlights problems in schools and society that need to be addressed, how can this perspective be developed or even sustained? The evidence that among educationally advantaged North Americans care focus is demonstrated primarily by girls and women raises questions about the relationship between female development and secondary education. But it also suggests that girls may constitute a resistance to the prevailing ethos of detachment and disconnection, a resistance that has moral and political as well as psychological implications. Thus the question arises as to how this resistance can be educated and sustained.

In tracing the development of women's thinking about what constitutes care and what connection means, I noted that a critical junction for women had to do with their inclusion of themselves (Gilligan, 1982). This inclusion is genuinely problematic, not only psychologically for women but also for society in general and for the secondary school curriculum. As self-inclusion on the part of women challenges the conventional understanding of feminine goodness by severing the link between care and self-sacrifice, so too the inclusion of women challenges the interpretive categories of the Western tradition, calling into question the description of human nature and holding up for scrutiny the meanings commonly given to relationship, love, morality, and self.

Perhaps for this reason, high school girls describing care focus dilemmas will say that their conflicts are not moral problems but just have to do with their lives and everything they believe in—as Anne said when she intimated that in fact she had another way of seeing the dilemma that she had posed in justice terms. From a care standpoint, her otherwise praiseworthy ability to say no to others seemed potentially problematic: What had seemed a valuable ability to stay centered in herself, to hold with what she believed, now seemed in part self-centered, a way of cutting herself off from the people around her. Thus development for girls in adolescence poses a conundrum, and at the center of this puzzle are questions about connection: How does one stay in touch with the world and others and with oneself? What are the possibilities for and the nature of genuine connection with others? What are the signs that distinguish true from false relationship? What leads girls to persist in seeking responsive engagement with others? What risks are attendant on this quest? And finally, what are the moral and political and psychological implications of resisting detachment? If one aim is to educate this resistance, secondary education may play a crucial role in this process.

Bardige (1983, 1985), analyzing the journals kept by seventh- and eighth-graders as part of the social studies curriculum, "Facing History and Ourselves: Holocaust and Human Behavior" by Strom and Parsons (1982), found evidence of moral sensibilities that seemed to be at risk in early adolescence. Specifically, she observed that the journal entries written by eight of the twenty-four girls and one of the nineteen boys in the two classes studied showed the children's willingness to take evidence of violence at face value, to respond directly to the perception that someone was being hurt. Because this responsiveness to evidence of violence was associated with less sophisticated forms of reasoning and because detachment and dispassion were linked with the ability to see both sides of a story and to reflect on the multiple lenses through which one can view or present a set of events, the tension between responsiveness and detachment poses an educational dilemma: How can one develop moral sensibilities anchored in common-sense perception while at the same time developing the capacity for logical thinking and reflective judgment? The present skewing of the secondary school curriculum, both in the humanities and the sciences, toward reasoning from premises and deductive logic, the emphasis placed on critical thinking, defined as the ability to think about thinking in the abstract, leaves uneducated or undeveloped the moral sensibilities that rely on a finely tuned perception—the ability to take one's reponses to what is taken in by seeing and listening as evidence on which to recognize false premises, as grounds for knowing what is happening and for thinking about what to do.

Given the heightened self-consciousness of teenagers and their intense fear of ridicule or exposure, secondary education poses a major challenge to teachers: How to sustain among teenagers an openness to experience and a willingness to risk discovery? The responsiveness of the relationship between teacher and student, the extent to which such connections involve a true engagement or meeting of minds, may be crucial in this regard. Yet when reliance on human resources is construed as a sign of limitation and associated with childhood dependence, the ways in which people can and do help one another tend not to be accurately represented. As a result, activities of care may be tacit or covertly undertaken or associated with idealized images of virtue and self-sacrifice. This poses a problem for teachers, parents, and adolescents, one which, for a variety of reasons, may fall particularly heavily on girls.

Psychologists recently have sought to understand the terms in which girls and women speak about their experience and have drawn attention to terms of relationship that suggest both a desire for responsive engagement with others and an understanding of what such connection entails (see Belenky and others, 1986; Josselson, 1987; Miller, 1984, 1986; Surrey, 1984). In addition, Steiner-Adair (1986), studying the vulnerability of high-school-age girls to eating disorders, found that girls who articulate a critical care perspective in response to interview questions about their own future expectations and societal values for women are invulnerable to eating disorders, as measured by the Eating Attitudes Test. The critical care perspective provided a standpoint from which to reject the assumptions embodied in the media image of the superwoman—assumptions that link separation and independence with success both in work and in love. Steiner-Adair found that in the educationally advantaged North American population where eating disorders currently are prevalent, girls who implicitly or explicitly take on or endorse the superwoman image, who do not identify a conflict between responsiveness in relationships and conventional images of femininity or of success, are those who appear vulnerable to eating disorders. Thus girls who show signs of vulnerability to eating disorders seem to be caught within a damaging framework of interpretation; when discussing their own future wishes and societal values, they do not differentiate signs of responsiveness and connection from images of perfection and control.

Along similar lines, Attanucci (1984) and Willard (1985), studying educationally advantaged North American mothers of young children, noted a disparity between mothers' own terms in speaking about their experiences as mothers and the terms used to characterize mothers and mothering in contemporary cultural scripts. Mothers' own terms included terms of relationships that convey mothers' experience of connection with their children, so that caring for children is neither selfish nor selfless in these terms. In contrast, the terms used by psychologists to describe good or good enough mothers convey the impression that women, insofar as they are good mothers, respond to their children's needs rather than to their own, whereas women, insofar as they are psychologically mature and healthy persons, meet their own needs and separate themselves from their children. Willard found that mothers who draw on their own experience of connection with their child in making decisions about work and family (whatever the specific nature of these decisions) do not suffer from symptoms of depression. In contrast, women who cast employment decisions in terms derived from cultural scripts, whether for good mothers or for superwomen, show signs of depression, suggesting that cultural scripts for mothers at present are detrimental to women. What differentiates these scripts for mothering from mothers' own terms is the division made between the woman herself and her child, so that mothers in essence are portrayed as caught between themselves and their child. The ability of adolescent girls and adult women to define connection and care in terms that reflect experiences of authentic relationship or responsive engagement with others and that encourage inclusive solutions to conflicts was associated in these three different studies by Steiner-Adair, Attanucci, and Willard with resistance to psychological illness—with invulnerability to eating disorders and the absence of depressive symptoms.

But the importance of reconsidering what is meant by care and connection as well as what responsiveness in relationship entails is underscored also by recent studies of inner-city youth (see Gilligan and others, 1985; Ward, 1986). The ability of teenagers living in the inner city to reason about care was often far more advanced than the level of their justice reasoning. In addition they often spoke clearly about the necessity for care and the reliance of people on human resources. For example, a fifteen-year-old, when asked to describe a moral conflict he had faced, spoke of a time when he wanted to go out with his friends after a dance but his mother wanted him home. He decided to go home, he said, to avoid "getting into trouble with my mother." However, when asked if he thought he had done the right thing, he spoke about the fact that he knew, from watching what had happened when his older sister stayed out late, that his mother would not sleep until he came home. His reason for going home was not simply grounded in a desire to avoid punishment (Stage I reasoning in Kohlberg's terms) but also in a wish not to hurt his mother and not to "just think about myself."

> My mother would have been worried about me all night if I stayed out. . . . [When] my sister used to do it to her, she didn't get any sleep all night. . . . I would be pretty bad if I kept her up like that, you know, just thinking about myself and not thinking about her. . . . Why should I just go off and not worry about her and just think about myself?

Hearing this teenager's concerns about avoiding punishment and getting into trouble, the psychologist schooled in the conventions of developmental psychology might well suspend further questioning, assuming a match with a codable low-level classification, a match rendered plausible because of this teenager's low socioeconomic status. Yet when the researcher, perhaps rejecting a Stage I depiction of a fifteen-year-old as implausible, chooses another line of questioning and pursues the boy's recognition that his actions can hurt his mother, the boy's moral strengths appear. He expresses concern about hurting his mother, and his awareness of how he can do so reveals a care perspective. Furthermore, his knowledge of what actions will cause hurt is based on his observations. Thus he does not need to put himself in his mother's place (which would earn him a higher score on stages of social, moral, and ego development) because he knows from experience with his mother how she will feel.

The change in assessment that follows from listening for two voices in the moral conflicts related by inner-city teenagers is further illustrated by a twelve-year-old girl who, asked for an example of moral conflict and choice, described a decision she made to override her mother's rules (Gilligan and others, 1985). Having laid out the moral world in terms of a stark contrast between "good guys" and "bad guys," she also contrasted this familiar moral language with the language of necessity. "Good guys," she explained, sustaining both languages, "know what's wrong and what's right and when to do right, and they know when it's necessary to do wrong." Her example of moral conflict involved precisely this judgment. A neighbor who had cut herself badly called because she needed bandages; the twelve-year-old had been told by her mother that she was not to leave the house. Discussing her decision to leave, she speaks repeatedly of the fact that she had to, referring to the neighbor's need and to her own judgment that it was absolutely necessary to help: "She needed my help so much, I helped her in any way I could. I knew that I was the only one who could help her, so I had to help her."

This example also contains a contrast between a seemingly simplistic moral conception (here a notion of absolute rules that determine right and wrong, irrespective of intention or motivation—a heteronomous morality in Piaget's terms or a low-stage morality in Kohlberg's terms) and a more sophisticated moral understanding, captured by the language of necessity—the need of people for help and the ability of people to help one another. Although the seeming inability of this girl to anticipate her mother's approval of her decision would qualify her for a low level of interpersonal perspective taking in Selman's (1980) terms, her insistence that "I did the right thing" and her belief that her actions would have been right even if her mother had disagreed with her decision suggests a more autonomous moral sense. Her decision in the instance she describes was guided by her judgment that help must be provided when it is needed and where it is possible: "You can't just stand there and watch the woman . . . die" (Gilligan and others, 1985). This disparity, between seemingly low stages of social and moral development, as measured by conventional psychological standards, and evidence of greater moral understanding and sensibilities than the developmental stage descriptions imply was encountered repeatedly in the study of inner-city teenagers, raising the kinds of questions about the moral life of children that have been articulated so pointedly by Coles (1986).

The implication of these studies, taken together, is that interpretive problems cannot be separated from the consideration of adolescent development and that these problems raise questions not only about adolescents but also about the society and culture in which these teenagers are coming of age. The observation often made by teachers that girls, in general, become less outspoken following puberty, less likely to disagree in public or even to participate in classroom discussions, together with the observation that school achievement tends to drop off in adolescence for the children of ethnic minorities suggest that secondary education, or the interpretive frameworks of the culture, may be more readily accessible and comprehensible to those students whose experience and background are most similar to that of those who shape the frameworks. If at present a care perspective offers a critical lens on a society that seems increasingly justice focused, it is also one that clarifies and makes sense of the activities of care that teenagers describe—not only helping others but also creating connections with others, activities they link with times when they feel good about themselves.

Gender differences along the same lines as those found among educationally advantaged teenagers were also observed among inner-city teenagers. Nine of eleven boys who described moral dilemmas involving friends focused their attention on the question of resisting peer pressure, while six of the ten girls whose dilemmas involved friends focused on questions of loyalty in relationship, citing as moral problems instances of abandonment, disconnection, and exclusion. In addition, girls in the inner city were more likely than boys to describe dilemmas that continued over time, rather than dilemmas portrayed as one-time occurrences or repeated instances of the same problem. Perhaps as a result, girls were more likely to seek inclusive solutions to the problems they described, solutions that contributed to sustaining and strengthening connections in that they were responsive to the needs of everyone involved. While girls were apt to talk about staying with a problem in relationships and with the people involved, boys were more likely to talk about leaving. The one boy in the study who described a continuing dilemma to which he sought an inclusive solution spoke about his problems in maintaining a relationship with both of his divorced parents. Thus the tendency to voice concerns about connection and to seek and value care and responsiveness in relationships was associated in these studies both with social class and with gender (see also Stack, 1974, and Ladner, 1972), like the findings reported by Johnston (1985) and Langdale (1983) that moral orientation, or the standpoint taken in solving moral problems, is associated both with gender and with the problem being considered.

The language of necessity that distinguishes the moral discourse of inner-city youths offers a compelling rendition of a care perspective in an environment characterized by high levels of violence. Ward's (1986) study of the ways in which adolescents living in the inner city think about the violence they witness in the course of their daily lives reveals the strengths of a focus on issues of care and connection—the association with nonviolent responses to violence and with holding off from violent response (often cast in the logic of retributive justice). Ward's study also reveals the importance accorded by teenagers to mothers who label violence in the family as violence (rather than speaking about love or not talking about what is happening) and who takes action to stop it. The clear sex differences with respect to violent action and the effects of these differences on male and female adolescents are curiously overlooked in current discussions about sex differences in moral development. Yet such differences pose major questions for theory and research.

Reconsidering adolescence from the two standpoints of justice and care and thinking about what constitutes development in both terms also spurs a reappraisal of traditional research methods, specifically a rethinking of the detachment that has been embedded in research practice. When interviewing pregnant teenagers who were considering abortion, I was struck by the fact that most of them knew about birth control. Their pregnancies seemed in part to have resulted from actions that comprised sometimes desperate, misguided, innocent strategies to care for themselves or others, to get what they wanted, or to avoid being alone. Engaging with these teenagers in the context of inquiring about their moral conflicts and interpretive quandaries raised a question about the effects of research as an intervention with both clinical and educational implications. What lessons are taught about connection and detachment, about care and justice, through the practice of asking teenagers, in the context of a research interview, about their experiences of moral conflict?

It may be that asking teenagers to talk about their own experiences of moral conflict and choice in itself constitutes an effective intervention, as some preliminary evidence suggests. Such questioning may reveal to teenagers that they have a moral perspective, something of value at stake, and thus that they have grounds for action in situations where they may have felt stuck or confused or unable to choose between alternative paths. The efficacy of the intervention may depend on the responsiveness of the research relationship, on whether the researcher engages with the teenager's thinking rather than simply mirroring or assessing it. For the adolescent, the realization that he, and perhaps especially she, has a moral perspective that an adult finds interesting, or a moral voice that someone will respond to, shifts the framework for action away from a choice between submission and rebellion (action defined in others' terms) and provides a context for discovering what are one's own terms. In adolescence, this discovery galvanizes energy and stimulates initiative and leadership.

But the same is true for teachers as well. The interpretive and ethical questions raised by considering adolescent development form a basis for genuine collaboration between psychologists and secondary school teachers. Such collaboration joins a naturalistic approach to research with what is perhaps the oldest strategy of education: not to teach answers but to raise questions that initiate the search for knowledge and, in the spirit of discovery, to listen for what is surprising. If the "modern" element in modern literature is the theme of disenchantment with the idea of culture or civilization, the challenge to those of us who would speak about development in adolescence, psychological health, or education is to take seriously the questions about truth and values that are raised by adolescents coming of age in modern culture and then, in responding to these questions, to imagine that this generation may hear different voices and may see from a new angle.

References

Adelson, J., and Doehrman, M. "The Psychodynamic Approach to Adolescence." In J. Adelson (ed.), *The Handbook of Adolescent Psychology*. New York: Wiley, 1980.

Arendt, H. *The Origins of Totalitarianism*. New York: Harcourt Brace Jovanovich, 1958.

Attanucci, J. "Mothers in Their Own Terms: A Developmental Perspective on Self and Role." Unpublished Ph.D. dissertation, Harvard Graduate School of Education, 1984.

Bardige, B. "Reflecting Thinking and Prosocial Awareness: Adolescents Face the Holocaust and Themselves." Unpublished Ph.D. dissertation, Harvard Graduate School of Education, 1983.

Bardige, B. "Things So Finely Human: Moral Sensibilities at Risk in Adolescence." Unpublished paper, Center for the Study of Gender, Education, and Human Development, Harvard Graduate School of Education, 1985.

Baumrind, D. "Parental Disciplinary Patterns and Social Competence in Children." *Youth and Society*, 1978, *9*, 239-276.

Belenky, M., Clinchy, B., Goldberger, N., and Traule, J. *Women's Ways of Knowing*. New York: Basic Books, 1986.

Bettelheim, B. "The Problem of Generations." *Daedalus*, 1961, *90*.

Blos, P. "The Second Individuation Process of Adolescence." *The Psychoanalytic Study of the Child*, 1967, *22*, 162-186.

Bowlby, J. *Attachment and Loss*. (3 vols.) New York: Basic Books, 1969, 1973, 1980.

Brown, L., Argyris, D., Attanucci, J., Bardige, B., Gilligan, C., Johnston, K., Miller, B., Osborne, R., Ward, J., and Wilcox, D. "A Guide to Reading Narratives of Moral Conflict and Choice for Self and Moral Voice." Unpublished manuscript, Center for the Study of Gender, Education, and Human Development, Harvard Graduate School of Education, 1987.

Chodorow, N. *The Reproduction of Mothering.* Berkeley: University of California Press, 1978.

Coles, R. *The Moral Life of Children.* Boston: Atlantic Monthly Press, 1986.

Emde, R. N., Johnson, W. F., and Easterbrooks, M. A. "The Do's and Dont's of Early Moral Development." In J. Kagan and S. Lamb (eds.), *The Emergence of Morality in Early Childhood.* Chicago: University of Chicago Press, 1987.

Erikson, E. *Young Man Luther.* New York: Norton, 1958.

Erikson, E. "Reflections on the Dissent of Humanist Youth." In E. Erikson (ed.), *Life History and the Historical Moment.* New York: Norton, 1975.

Freud, S. "Some Psychical Consequences of the Anatomical Differences Between the Sexes." In J. Strachey (ed.), *Complete Psychological Works of Sigmund Freud.* Vol. 19. London: Hogarth, 1961. (Originally published 1925.)

Gilligan, C. "In a Different Voice: Women's Conceptions of Self and of Morality." *Harvard Educational Review,* 1977, *47,* 481–517.

Gilligan, C. *In a Different Voice: Psychological Theory and Women's Development.* Cambridge, Mass.: Harvard University Press, 1982.

Gilligan, C. "Exit-Voice Dilemmas in Adolescence." In A. Foxley, M. McPherson, and G. O'Donnell (eds.), *Development, Democracy, and the Art of Trespassing: Essays in Honor of Albert O. Hirschman.* Notre Dame, Ind.: University of Notre Dame Press, 1986a.

Gilligan, C. "Remapping the Moral Domain: New Images of the Self in Relationship." In T. C. Heller, M. Sosna, and D. E. Wellbery (eds.), *Reconstructing Individualism.* Stanford, Calif.: Stanford University Press, 1986b.

Gilligan, D., and Attanucci, J. "Two Moral Orientations: Implications for Developmental Theory and Assessment." Unpublished paper, Center for the Study of Gender, Education, and Human Development, Harvard Graduate School of Education, 1985.

Gilligan, C., Bardige, B., Ward, J., Taylor, J., and Cohen, G. "Moral and Identity Development in Urban Youth." Report to the Rockefeller Foundation, 1985.

Gottman, J. M. "How Children Become Friends." *Society for Research in Child Development Monograph,* 1983, *48* (3), 1–86.

Hoffman, M. "Empathy, Role-Taking, Guilt, and the Development of Altruistic Motives." In T. Lickona (ed.), *Moral Development and Behavior.* New York: Holt, Rinehart & Winston, 1976.

Inhelder, B., and Piaget, J. *The Growth of Logical Thinking from Childhood to Adolescence.* New York: Basic Books, 1958.

Johnston, D. K. "Two Moral Orientations; Two Problem-Solving Strategies: Adolescents' Solutions to Dilemmas in Fables." Unpublished Ph.D. dissertation, Harvard Graduate School of Education, 1985.

Josselson, R. *Finding Herself: Pathways to Identify Development in Women.* San Francisco: Jossey-Bass, 1987.

Kagan, J. "A Conception of Early Adolescence." *Daedalus,* 1971, *100,* 997–1012.

Kagan, J. *The Nature of the Child.* New York: Basic Books, 1984.

Kohlberg, L. "Stage and Sequence." In D. Goslin (ed.), *Handbook of Socialization Theory and Research.* Chicago: Rand McNally, 1969.

Kohlberg, L., and Gilligan, C. "The Adolescent as a Philosopher." *Daedalus,* 1971, *100,* 1051–1086.

Konopka, G. *The Adolescent Girl in Conflict.* Englewood Cliffs, N.J.: Prentice-Hall, 1966.

Ladner, S. *Tomorrow's Tomorrow.* New York: Anchor Books, 1972.

Langdale, S. "Moral Orientation and Moral Development: The Analysis of Care and Justice Reasoning Across Different Dilemmas in Females and Males from Childhood Through Adulthood." Unpublished Ph.D. dissertation, Harvard Graduate School of Education, 1983.

Lightfoot, S. L. *The Good High School*. New York: Basic Books, 1983.

Lyons, N. P. "Two Perspectives: On Self, Relationships, and Morality." *Harvard Educational Review*, 1983, *53*, 125–146.

Miller, J. B. *Toward a New Psychology of Women*. Boston: Beacon Press, 1976.

Miller, J. B. "The Development of Women's Sense of Self." *Work in Progress*, no. 12. Wellesley, Mass.: Stone Center, 1984.

Miller, J. B. "What Do We Mean by Relationships?" *Work in Progress*, no. 22. Wellesley, Mass.: Stone Center, 1986.

Perry, W. *Forms of Intellectual and Ethical Development in the College Years*. New York: Holt, Rinehart & Winston, 1970.

Piaget, J. *The Moral Judgment of the Child*. New York: Free Press, 1965. (Originally published 1932.)

Pipp, S., Shaver, P., Jennings, S., Lamborn, S., and Fischer, K. "Adolescents' Theories About the Development of Relationships with Parents." *Journal of Personality and Social Psychology*, 1985, *48*, 991–1001.

Polanyi, M. *Personal Knowledge*. Chicago: University of Chicago Press, 1958.

Ravitch, D. "Decline and Fall of Teaching History." *New York Times Sunday Magazine*, November 17, 1985, p. 50.

Rutter, M., Maughan, B., Mortimore, P., Ouston, J., and Smith, A. *Fifteen Thousand Hours*. Cambridge, Mass.: Harvard University Press, 1979.

Selman, R. *The Growth of Interpersonal Understanding*. New York: Academic Press, 1980.

Stack, C. *All Our Kin*. New York: Harper & Row, 1974.

Steiner-Adair, C. "The Body Politic: Normal Female Adolescent Development and the Development of Eating Disorders." *Journal of the American Academy of Psychoanalysis*, 1986, *14* (1), 95–114.

Stern, D. *The Interpersonal World of the Infant*. New York: Basic Books, 1985.

Strom, M., and Parsons, W. *Facing History and Ourselves: Holocaust and Human Behavior*. Watertown, Mass.: International Education, 1982.

Surrey, J. "The Self-in-Relation." *Work in Progress*, no. 13. Wellesley, Mass.: Stone Center, 1984.

Trilling, L. "On the Modern Element in Modern Literature." In I. Howe (ed.), *The Idea of the Modern in Literature and the Arts*. New York: Horizon Press, 1967.

Vygotsky, L. *Mind in Society*. Cambridge, Mass.: Harvard University Press, 1978.

Ward, J. "A Study of Urban Adolescents' Thinking About Violence Following a Course on the Holocaust." Unpublished Ph.D. dissertation, Harvard Graduate School of Education, 1986.

Willard, A. K. "Self, Situation, and Script: A Psychological Study of Decisions About Employment in Mothers of One-Year-Olds." Unpublished Ph.D. dissertation, Harvard Graduate School of Education, 1985.

Youniss, J., and Smollar, J. *Adolescents' Relations with Mothers, Fathers, and Friends*. Chicago: University of Chicago Press, 1985.

Further Sources

Adelson, J. (ed.). *The Handbook of Adolescent Psychology*. New York: Wiley, 1980.

Brown, L. "When Is a Moral Problem Not a Moral Problem?" Unpublished manuscript, Harvard Graduate School of Education, 1986.

92

Gilligan, C. "The Conquistador and the Dark Continent: Reflections on the Psychology of Love." *Daedalus,* 1984, *113,* 75–95.

Gilligan, C. "Reply." *Signs,* 1986, *11* (2), 324–333.

Gilligan, C., and Wiggins, G. "The Origins of Morality in Early Childhood Relationships." In J. Kagan and S. Lamb (eds.), *The Emergence of Morality in Early Childhood.* Chicago: University of Chicago Press, 1987.

Kohlberg, L. *Education for Justice: A Modern Statement of the Platonic View.* Cambridge, Mass.: Harvard University Press, 1968.

Konopka, G. *Young Girls: A Portrait of Adolescents.* Englewood Cliffs, N.J.: Prentice-Hall, 1976.

Osborne, R. "Good-Me, Bad-Me, True-Me, False-Me: A Dynamic Multidimensional Study of Adolescent Self-Concept." Unpublished Ph.D. dissertation, Harvard Graduate School of Education, 1987.

Wiggins, G. "Thoughtfulness as an Educational Aim." Unpublished Ph.D. dissertation, Harvard Graduate School of Education, 1986.

*Carol Gilligan is professor of education at Harvard University.
Her major research interest is moral development in
adolescence.*

*Adolescent risk-taking behavior must be understood in the
context of contemporary youth culture and normal
development. To facilitate secure passage through the
adolescent transition, parents should sustain a climate
of control and commitment balanced by respect for the
adolescent's increased capacity for self-regulation.*

A Developmental Perspective on Adolescent Risk Taking in Contemporary America

Diana Baumrind

In the mid 1970s, a growing public concern about the health and welfare
of America's young people gave rise to a myriad of conferences, commis-
sion reports, and special issues of scholarly journals devoted to the prob-
lems of youth in America. The commission reports included the Panel on
Youth of the President's Science Advisory Committee, known as Coleman
II (Coleman, 1974), the National Commission on the Reform of Secondary
Education established by the Kettering Foundation (Brown, 1973), and the
National Panel on High School and Adolescent Education (National
Panel . . . , 1976). Critiques included an entire issue of the *School Review*

During the preparation of this chapter, the author was supported by a
Research Scientist Award (number 1-K05-MH00485-01) and a research grant
(number 1-R01-MH38343-01) from the National Institute of Mental Health. During
the adolescent phase of the research, the project was supported by research grant
(number 1-R01-DA01919) from the National Institute on Drug Abuse, and by one
from the John D. and Catherine T. MacArthur Foundation. The William T. Grant
Foundation has provided consistent and generous support of this longitudinal
program of research, including the present phase of analysis of the early adolescent
data (supported by grant number 84044973).

C. E. Irwin, Jr. (ed.). *Adolescent Social Behavior and Health.*
New Directions for Child Development, no. 37. San Francisco: Jossey-Bass, Fall 1987.

(Wright, 1974) devoted to the Coleman II report, a series of reports on national youth policy issued by the Social Research Group of George Washington University (Heyneman, 1976a, 1976b), and a scholarly commentary on youth policy in transition prepared by the Rand Foundation (Timpane, Abramowitz, Bobrow, and Pascal, 1976). The consensus in the 1970s was that young people were victims of social forces beyond their control and that their challenge to the established order was justified. Over the past decade, although public concern about the same set of social-behavioral problems has not abated, the problems themselves have been relabeled as risk-taking behavior, thereby implying that young people are less the victims of a disordered society than the source of problems that they themselves create.

Despite these fluctuations in the way we have historically viewed the causes of such problematic behavior, it remains possible to distinguish between risk-taking propensities that are characteristic of the adolescent stage of development and the objective conditions that place contemporary youth at risk. For example, the fact that 60 percent of black children have no father in the home (Moynihan, 1986) poses a threat to these children and to their single mothers, many of whom are children themselves. But the cause of their predicament lies less in the risk-taking propensities of black adolescent girls than in such social factors as the inability of young black men to find employment. Since motherhood provides a rite of passage into the world of adult work, pregnancy may be construed by many black adolescents not as an undesirable accidental or risk-taking endeavor, but as a worthwhile achievement. Suicide, the third leading cause of death among youths fifteen to twenty-four years of age, and a special threat to American Indian males, is the ultimate expression not of risk-seeking but rather of despair and withdrawal. Similarly, health-endangering eating disorders such as anorexia and obesity are maladaptive coping strategies, but they are not undertaken with risk in mind.

However, when all has been said, it must be acknowledged that it is matter of great social concern that dangerous behaviors with few compensatory benefits such as drug use, promiscuous sex, reckless driving, and delinquency, have become normative features of our contemporary youth culture, accepted and even admired rather than rejected and deplored. We should seek to understand why so many young people today fail to avoid, or consciously seek, experiences that adults and many young people themselves perceive to be personally and socially destructive.

Youth Culture

In order to address the self-inflicted causes of adolescents' failure to thrive, it is necessary to understand contemporary youth culture, since individual development is necessarily conditioned by secular events. By youth culture I refer to the shared meanings and coherent set of issues that define the sociomoral ecology of youth in a given era. In claiming to consider these issues from a developmental perspective, I mean that I am concerned with the factors operative in a given society that facilitate or interfere with movement toward optimal human functioning. Development is viewed as a process characterized by alternating periods of relative disequilibrium and equilibrium, in which the global and diffuse organization of ontogenetically primitive discrete schemes of action become increasingly differentiated, integrated, more coherent, and better adapted to specific demand characteristics of the environment.

Contemporary American society is quite different from that of the 1960s. The extreme anti-authority attitudes prevalent among young people in the 1960s were a direct reaction to the Vietnam war and were supported by the widespread affluence and confidence that came with an expanding economy. LSD, which was first synthesized in 1938, became widely available, and its use was sanctified by the charismatic Timothy Leary. The 1960s brought national innocence to an end and the withdrawal of naive trust in designated authorities such as government officials, college professors, and other professional experts. The constellation of problem behaviors in the 1960s reflected not merely an ethos of immediate gratification but constituted also a political statement about young people's relationship to discredited authority. As respect for authority diminished in all strata of society, the illegality of many risk-taking acts lost its value as either a practical or a moral deterrent.

The 1970s marked a transitional period, a coming down from the economic and emotional high of the 1960s. Adolescents experiencing the anticipatory stress of entering the constricted labor market of the 1970s were less likely to value countercultural risk-taking for its own sake. Such adolescent problem behaviors as drug use and premature sexual activity became conventional recreations rather than exotic or ideological pursuits. In the 1970s both the hard work society demanded and the payoffs it provided were questioned by the young. Yankelovich (1981) attributes the breakdown in traditions, and the despair and alienation that afflicted so many, to a permanent reduction in the material standard of living brought about by increased costs of energy, defense, and entitlement programs and to a decline in the competitiveness of American industry.

Contemporary American socioeconomic and sociomoral realities impact unfavorably on youthful development in at least two ways:

First, in the United States today, adolescents are effectively excluded from adult society and have no normative niche of their own. The gap between puberty and psychosocial maturity is wider than ever before and is likely to remain so, since puberty is reached at an earlier age today than it was in the past and the sagging economy cannot employ all the young people the society produces. Thus, entry into the adult world of commitment and responsibility is often delayed for affluent youth and may be permanently denied to a growing proportion of the poor. Erikson (1968) believes that if society grants the adolescent a moratorium, a time to explore and experiment safely, the identity crisis will be resolved in a stable sense of identity. However, contemporary American society provides few of its adolescents with a moratorium. Affluent adolescents construct their reality in a social matrix that often appears so malleable that it is experienced as hypothetical and unreal rather than as challenging, whereas the social matrix in which poor youths construct their reality is often so intransigent and moribund that it provides them with a mortuary rather than a moratorium.

Second, the social role of women has been permanently altered in ways that place them at greater risk themselves and make them less able to perform their traditional moderating function as conservators of health. The special status that accompanied the role of martyred mother is gone forever. The changes brought about by the women's movement—no matter how liberating they have been—do have at least these expectably negative consequences for adolescent development: First, to the extent that maternal presence in the home has been an essential part of traditional upbringing, the conservative and countervailing force exerted by tradition will be diminished. Second, the benefits provided by the presence of an adult in the home to supervise the activities of adolescents and to provide them with comfort and solace will be lost. Third, young women will be likely to engage in increasingly greater risk-taking problem behavior symbolic of their liberated status. Women's use of tobacco and their involvement in acts of violence, relative to men, has already increased in the last decade.

Generativity through work and procreation are no longer of clear positive value. Unless a new set of values can be found on which to base new traditions, adolescents will lack a socially sanctioned ego ideal to form the core of a positive identity. Yankelovich (1981) perceives the emergence of just such a new social ethic. He asserts that in contrast to the utopian dropout mentality of the 1960s or the narcissistic self-centeredness of the 1970s, an ethic of commitment has emerged in the 1980s. He suggests that the frenetic search of individual self-actualization of the two previous decades is yielding to a search for fulfillment through meaningful personal relationships and enduring commitments to work and community service.

What Yankelovich calls an ethic of self-fulfillment through commitment Gilligan refers to as a "different voice" (1982), and Lenz and Myerhoff (1985) call the feminization of America. Lenz and Myerhoff claim that woman's historic responsibility for protecting life has endowed her with such adaptive characteristics as a strong nurturing impulse toward all living things, a highly developed capacity for intimacy and empathy, a tendency to integrate rather than separate, and a scale of values that places individual growth and fulfillment above abstractions. Not all agree that these are feminine values or that their influence is becoming pervasive in American culture.

However, there is interesting evidence that an ethic of commitment and concern is emerging in the youth culture of the 1980s in the socially conscious leadership role assumed by the heroes of popular culture. If there is a resurgence of political consciousness among popular youth heroes, it may help combat the sense of alienation that fuels dysfunctional risk-taking behavior.

Normal Adolescent Development

Our culture has no rites of passage to demarcate the change in status from child to adult, but it has instead a long transitional period that we call adolescence. By adolescence I refer to an age span roughly between ages ten and twenty-five that is heralded by the accelerating physical changes accompanying puberty; results in sexual maturity and identity formation; and eventuates in emancipation from childhood dependency and crucial decisions concerning school, love, and work. Adolescence is a psychosocial stage in the life span and therefore specific to class and culture. Ages 10 to 15, which are often used to bracket early adolescence, correspond to the ages of children attending middle schools and junior high schools in the United States. Ages 15 to 18, which bracket midadolescence, correspond to the ages of children attending high schools. Late adolescence then extends from high school graduation to entry into one or more adult roles, establishing a pattern of interdependence in love and work settings such that the youth is functioning either as an interdependent rather than a dependent member of the family of origin or alternatively independent of it.

Adolescence is a period of development involving transitions in physical, intellectual, psychosocial, and moral processes. In order to progress from one developmental stage to the next, a disequilibrating conflict must occur that motivates the individual to abandon the comfort of a well-integrated state of reasoning or lifeview for a new and, therefore, less secure stance. The adolescent identity crisis is a disequilibrating conflict during which adolescents question the heretofore accepted values of their parents and other adult authorities before arriving at a set of principles capable of reconciling the disparate points of view characterizing their own and their parents' generations. Patterns of childrearing that discourage dissent by restricting adolescents' range of experiences may reduce their risk-taking behavior but at the cost of distorting and delaying the process of identity formation and emancipation. Adolescents who do not undergo a process of emancipation in some form are said to have a "foreclosed identity" (Erikson, 1959): They remain willing pawns of others, unwilling to accept responsibility for the consequences of their actions.

Early adolescence vies with infancy as a period of most rapid biopsychosocial growth. By definition, a transitional period such as adolescence is disequilibrating and disrupting and thus replete with opportunities for experiences that are both dangerous and growth enhancing. But there are asynchronies in the biological, social, emotional, and intellectual levels of maturity achieved at a given time by a particular adolescent, as well as individual differences in overall rate of maturation. These intraindividual and interindividual differences necessarily qualify the stage-related description of early adolescence that follows. The psychosocial processes that define adolescence should be viewed as paths to be negotiated rather than as naturally evolving growth patterns that automatically affect all adolescents similarly.

Risk-taking behavior characterizes normal adolescent development. The pursuit of opportunities for self-transcendent challenge (eustress), and pleasurable excess (eudaemonism), when moderated by an ethic of care and commitment, can be associated with secondary gains such as higher self-confidence, increased stress tolerance, and practice in taking initiative. It is important—not only for researchers but also for parents—to distinguish between such normal transitional risk-taking behaviors that though dangerous are developmentally adaptive and those pathological expressions for which secondary gains are virtually absent. Although a prima facie case can be made that certain kinds of early adolescent behavior that deviate from adult standards as, for example, regular substance use (see Baumrind and Moselle, 1985) and sexual activity have health-endangering consequences, these same behaviors may simultaneously accompany healthy, mature personality development. Thus, in a socially advantaged middle-class population such as the one I am studying, the personal antecedents at age 9 of adolescent marijuana experimentation were uniformly indicative of social maturity, demonstrating that such risk-taking behavior is not pathological although it may be pathogenic (Baumrind, 1985). Clearly, heroin addiction or teenage pregnancy have little to recommend them and serve to foreclose rather than to explore options. But some experimentation—be it with drugs or sex or odd diets or new ideas—is typical, and may even be an essential component, of a healthful adolescent experience and contribute to optimal competence. By optimal competence, I mean a coordination or integration within the person of the socially responsible and agentic modes of behavior. (Agentic, as used in this chapter, refers to persons who are doers, or leaders, or who are capable of being agents of change for themselves.)

Early adolescence is a period of heightened consciousness of self and others, resulting simultaneously in enhanced ability to understand the perspective of another and in increased self-centeredness. Greater self-consciousness becomes possible as a result of adolescents' increasing ability to engage in recursive thought, that is, to treat as objects of contemplation both their own thoughts and the thoughts of others. The acquisition of mature role-taking skills occurs in early adolescence. Selman (1971, 1980) believes that social perspective taking follows an invariant stage sequence. During early adolecence, youths construct an understanding of the shared perspective among individuals that exists in particular social groupings. Such a construction permits them to compare and contrast viewpoints of the self, specific others, and the generalized other.

As a result, adolescents can conceive of health and illness in terms of multiple causes, and educators can use adolescents' developing awareness of their own physiological states to teach them how to monitor their physical and mental health. Elkind (1967a) emphasizes the opposite side of adolescents' increased capacity for role taking: their egocentrism and sense of being altogether unique. Many adolescents, confronted for the first time with an awareness of their objectification in the minds of others and overwhelmed by associated feelings of self-consciousness, use their emerging cognitive abilities to construct a personal fable reaffirming their specialness and separateness.

Lowered self-esteem presents a special risk to young adolescents, with stabilization in self-ideal congruence beginning around the ninth grade and recovery occurring by age 18 (Bachman, Green, and Wirtanen, 1971; Jorgensen and Howell, 1969; Nickols, 1963; Yamamoto, Thomas, and Karnes, 1969). Dramatic discontinuities in body image occur as a result of pubertal changes, so that youngsters may actually be less physically attractive at precisely that time at which their awareness of self and others is developing. A decrease in self-ideal congruence and self-esteem occurs between ages 8 and 13 together with a downward trend in the sense of self-worth. High-achieving youths may be especially susceptible to decreased self-esteem. In 1961 Coleman observed that among adolescents, leading social cliques tended to discourage academic strivings, and this fact may not have changed substantially in the past quarter of a century. Superior school achievement may still reduce rather than enhance one's popularity with peers (Gordon, 1972). As the importance of parental approval wanes with the increasing importance of peer approbation, high-achievers can be faced with a dilemma—namely, that the approval of their age mates may be based not so much on high academic achievement as on conformity to group standards of behavior, standards that the high-achiever may at first be reluctant to adopt. However, if these youths fail to meet their own high academic standards or if they suffer the rejection of their peers, the high-achiever may then seek solace in groups that by adult standards, are deviant.

The accelerated cognitive development of early adolescence, second only to the rate of infant growth, is as much a function of the complexity of new social tasks to be mastered as of biological growth. In order to advance cognitively to formal operational thought, disequilibrating conflicts on beliefs and relationships must occur. Cognitive dissonance arising from interpersonal conflicts can encourage adolescents to take the role of others with divergent understandings and values. Parents' willingness and ability to allow conflictual interchange to develop and be resolved, while sustaining an affective climate of support and mutual respect should facilitate cognitive development during adolescence (Powers and others, 1983), at least in youths who are not regular drug users.

The acquisition of formal operations enables some adolescents to negotiate the transition from conventional to principled morality. However, not all adolescents or adults acquire formal operations or require them to accomplish their daily tasks. Adolescents from middle-class professional homes are most likely to acquire formal operations. Adolescents who do acquire formal operations can systematically hypothecate possibilities that run counter to fact and can critique the status quo for being but one possible social arrangement and not necessarily the most satisfactory one, a perspective Kohlberg and Gilligan (1972) refer to as "cultural relativism." They can coherently employ internally consistent logical operations both to comprehend observed regularities in the environment and to critique the way it functions. From a position not yet constrained by the social realities of adult commitment and responsibility such adolescents may freely critique the imperfection and hypocrisy of their parents' generation.

In giving up a view of parental authority as absolute and unquestionably valid, adolescents in the process of emancipation do not typically develop a negative identity that totally rejects parental values en masse. Instead, adolescent negation of convention usually expresses simultaneous emulation and rejection of parental standards. For example, in emulation of their elders, adolescents use drugs to assuage immediate or anticipated discomfort, and in rejection of their elders, they seize on certain drugs of which their elders disapprove. The use of illicit substances offers young adolescents an opportunity to rebel against the rules their elders set down while simultaneously conforming with underlying parental attitudes.

Turiel (1978) identified seven levels of social-conventional concepts through analyses of children's and adolescents' responses to a probing (Piagetian) clinical interview. He found that prior to ages 12 or 13, adherence to convention is based on concrete rules and authoritative expectations. Later, with the early adolescent transition (to Turiel's fourth stage), children typically come to question parental authority and social expectation as bases for following convention. Conventions that serve to maintain the dominant social order but that are not seen as intrinsically good (such as dress codes) tend to be viewed as arbitrary, and therefore rules or laws supporting such conventions are asserted to be invalid. From ages 14 to 16, with the transition to Turiel's fifth stage, systematic concepts of social structure typically emerge, and adult-supported conventions are once again affirmed, now however justified by their regulative function, with the proviso that the social order is itself viewed as legitimate.

Increased symmetry of power typically characterizes family structure following puberty. During childhood, power is asymmetrical in the family unit. As Dubin and Dubin (1963) point out, by experiencing the imposition of parental authority in the early years, children learn to express their social individuality within the confines of what the culture will accept. However, power cannot be used by parents to legitimate or enforce their authority once the young person acquires formal operational thought. While head-on confrontation may serve to strengthen parental authority in the authority inception period, negotiation and intellectual exchange are more effective during adolescence. A renegotiation of entitlements and obligations among family members following puberty is appropriate and should enable adolescents to accept reasonable parental control.

Beginning in early adolescence, the peer group becomes increasingly significant as a socializing context, but the effect of the family, though diminished, is by no means eradicated. Adolescents comply with peer standards up to a point to achieve status and identity within the peer group. Peer influence predicts initiation to alcohol and marijuana, and the influence of a best friend may lead to the initiation of other illicit drugs (Kandel, Kessler, and Margulies, 1978). However, influence on long-range educational aspirations and occupational plans appears to remain the province of parents (Douvan and Adelson, 1966; Brittain, 1968), and family environment variables predict later adverse outcomes in school or with the police (Langner and others, 1983). Adults in our society can use socialization contexts, including the peer group, to reinforce health-maintaining values just as adults in collectivized societies manipulate the adolescent peer group to reinforce the dominant communal views of their society (Bronfenbrenner, 1970, 1972, 1979; Kessen, 1975). Indeed important changes in adolescents' attitudes toward smoking have been brought about by just such effective adult manipulation of the media and educational contexts. If dependency on peers relative to parents has increased over the last twenty-five years, it is not because parents lack the ability to be influential but rather because parents have chosen to withdraw from the lives of their youngsters. Such withdrawal creates an emptiness in the life of adolescents and a fertile ground for the growth of feelings of abandonment and alienation.

Issues of alienation and commitment are central to understanding adolescent risk-taking behavior. The term *alienation* is often thought of in a political context. The early Marx, ([1844] 1964, [1858] 1971) for example, critiqued capitalist society because it alienated workers from the fruits of their labor and deprived them of moral autonomy. However, the notion of alienation has its roots in spiritual thought. Humans, originally one with God, by their recalcitrance alienate themselves and then, as they become enlightened, progressively work themselves back to God. The mystic experience of dissolving personal boundaries in merging with the beloved or of becoming one with the universe through meditation has always been valued for its own sake.

Alienation also describes a psychological state in which a human being feels like an outsider in the community, unable to find a shared interest and a consensually validated way to contribute to society. The component negative attitudes that constitute psychological alienation include normlessness, or the belief that socially disapproved behaviors are required to achieve one's goals; isolation, or the belief that one's personal goals are misunderstood, rejected, or not rewarded by society; and meaninglessness, or the withdrawal of value attribution from one's acts.

From a sociological perspective, adolescents are in fact outsiders in modern Western societies. Keniston (1965) popularized the term *alienation* to describe the malaise of middle-class youth in the 1960s. Young people contemplating entrance as workers into an economy in which basic economic processes are reified and depersonalized are prone to feel helpless, estranged, and alienated. If adolescents cannot see their own interests and needs reflected in external social norms, compliance with such norms becomes equated with estrangement from the self, entailing a sacrifice of the self to society. Conversely, when adolescents cannot or will not recognize the extent to which social conventions inevitably mediate their perceptions of what they view as intrinsic personal characteristics, their personal lives become alienated from the collective. Unless an ethic of private fulfillment and radical autonomy is balanced by an ethic of civic commitment and interpersonal caring, a sense of alienation inevitably results (Bellah and others, 1985). Once the adolescent recognizes a reciprocal relationship between spontaneous self-interest and social conformity, the risk of estrangement from the self or from society is attenuated, and genuine intersubjective encounters become possible.

In sum, the attainment of sexual maturation and full stature signaled by puberty liberates adolescents and their parents from the asymmetrical dependence-nurturance bond of childhood. The cognitive and moral advances accompanying puberty enable adolescents to conceive of themselves as individuated and self-regulating beings. Capable now of hypothecating possibilities beyond the concrete experiences of their past, adolescents may construct a moral vision of an ideal world in which inequities are resolved justly and peers nourish and care for each other in mutual love and interdependence. These new potentialities for critical ideation and action enable adolescents to develop enduring commitments to lovers, work, and transcendent ideals but also place adolescents at risk in contemporary America. Unlike traditional societies, which offer guidelines to human behavior that remain relevant across many generations, contemporary American society presents adolescents with contradictory and diffuse values, extreme mobility, and a dearth of extended support groups. Premature rejection of, or ejection from, the protective environment of the family further increases the risk of anomie, confusion, and alienation. The amotivational syndrome describes a pattern of apathetic withdrawal of energy and interest from effortful activity, an uncertainty about long-range goals with resultant mental and physical lethargy, a loss of creativity, and social withdrawal from demanding social stimuli. These symptoms, descriptive of adolescent alienation, have also been associated with youthful substance abuse, which in turn is a prototypic symptom, as well as a probable cause, of adolescent alienation.

Adolescent Substance Abuse

The past two decades have seen an unprecedented increase in the abuse of alcohol and drugs by adolescents. Indeed drug experimentation has become a normative rite of passage in our society. In two earlier papers (Baumrind, 1985; Baumrind and Moselle, 1985), we presented a prima facie case against recreational and chronic early adolescent drug use and posited specific negative consequences, including impairment of attention and memory; developmental lag in cognitive, moral, and psychosocial domains; amotivational syndrome; consolidation of diffuse or negative identity; and social alienation and estrangement.

The abuse of psychotropic drugs is implicated in adolescent alienation and estrangement in at least four ways: (1) Drug abuse may interfere in general with a process of personal identity formation such that a sense of personal continuity becomes antithetical to identification with others; (2) more specifically, drug abuse results from and contributes to a break in the intergenerational continuity both in the transmission of values and in the maintenance of viable parent-child relationships; (3) the phantasmic perception of social reality induced by the drug experience may be preserved in a generalized world view based on little actual engagement with the world; and (4) the social consequences of drug abuse may confirm the sense of vulnerability, powerlessness, and external locus of control—feelings that may have led to drug abuse in the first place.

1. Failure to develop a sense of personal identity capable of reconciling the spontaneous expression of self-interest with externally imposed constraints leaves the adolescent caught between two poles of a dialectic in which alienation is an inevitable by-product. That failure has its roots in familial dysfunction and childhood pathology. However, involvement with drugs and a drug subculture interferes further with the process of constructing a social identity by engendering an egocentric focus on personal desires and intentions. Distortions of consciousness are likely to impair adolescents' social understanding and generate a paradoxical situation where abusers essentially give themselves over unreflectively to the binding force of peer group social norms while believing that they are pursuing

their own individualistic ends. Thus drug users may appear to be socially assertive as they were in our study ($r = 0.18$ between amount of drug use by adolescents and their scores on a factor appropriately named Social Agency) but fall easily under peer influence. Conversely, identifying with peer reference group norms and untempered by a simultaneous consideration of their own subjective motives and intentions, drug abusing adolescents may pursue a course of social interaction in a largely egocentric, idiosyncratic manner while believing that they have internalized a body of consensually validated norms. Engaged in a practice that conceals individuality while reducing thoughts, feelings, actions—and ultimately persons—to the effects of the drug, adolescents may fail to acquire the shared perspective among individuals that arises precisely through the effort to comprehend the idiosyncrasies of others viewed as active, responsible agents in their own right. At the same time, the values of the drug subculture that the adolescent has joined continue to exert a socializing force that is untempered by reflection.

2. The manner in which identity is preserved at the expense of engagement with others is illustrated clearly in the relationships of parents and drug-using adolescents. Interactions between drug-using adolescents and their nonusing parents and friends become awkward and lacking in mutuality, accounting in part for the desire of drug-takers to turn on their nonusing friends. Even parents who have experimented with drugs themselves will be unable to share their adolescents' experience, since the drug experience is affected dramatically by the stage of development of the user and the setting in which the drug is used. Since drugs may be used to facilitate emancipation from parents, adolescents may at first welcome the break. However, parent-child relationships may then deteriorate rapidly as a result of the clash in values. By labeling the user as deviant and unworthy and by attempting to elicit conformity through coercion, parents may unwittingly help the adolescent to equate conformity with alienation. Evidence that drug use is associated with beliefs adults regard as deviant but that peers endorse comes from two sources in our study: First, the relation between amount of drug use and rejection of deviant attitudes on the Jessor Proscriptive Scale (Jessor and Jessor, 1974) was −0.51; and second, amount of drug use correlated *negatively* with endorsement of items on the Crandall Social Desirability Questionnaire (Crandall, Crandall, and Katkovsky, 1965) aimed at obtaining the approval of adults ($r = -0.39$) but *positively* with endorsement of items aimed at obtaining the approval of peers ($r = 0.37$).

3. The generalized world view produced by immersion in the drug experience and drug culture may consolidate the surreal state of consciousness characteristic of adolescents because it reflects their actual although temporary social status as marginal citizens. The subjective experiences produced by drugs separate affect from the encounters that normally gen-

erate affect, sensations from the stimuli that normally give rise to them, and the perceiving ego from the physical body and surrounding environment. By artificially manipulating the body image and altering the relations between self and environment, adolescent users may fail to achieve a stable body image and may obscure the differentiations of subject and object that enable persons to monitor external stimuli and to master their environment. Drug-induced states of mind are especially insidious because they frequently present themselves to the user as cosmic enlightment and not as a mere product of unreflective drug intoxication. Indeed drugs are valued because of how they alter consciousness and reduce achievement anxiety. As a result, drug-using adolescents may not rise to cognitive challenges and may lose interest in school. Our study includes striking evidence of the presence of a cognitive functional deficit in the large negative correlation between amount of marijuana use and the factor we call Cognitive Agency ($r = -0.51$), a factor defined by such variables as Challenges Self Intellectually, Strives for Excellence, Academic Motivation and Productivity. With little or no actual engagement or struggle, chronic drug intoxication can produce the illusion of autonomy and self-assertion while actually pacifying and immobilizing the user. The surreal state of consciousness produced by marijuana and psychedelic intoxication characteristically includes the following elements: a sense of being taken over rather than of being in charge; the loss of a future time perspective and devaluation of the past; concern with experiencing rather than with doing; an ethic of personal gratification at the expense of social welfare; and a focus on freedom and noncommitment.

4. A sense of vulnerability, powerlessness, and external locus of control are developmentally normal and appropriate to adolescents' in-limbo social status. However, as a direct extension of the drug experience and as an indirect consequence of the devaluing of that experience and of the drug-using youths themselves by members of powerful reference groups, these developmentally normal states may be intensified or consolidated in enduring fatalism, alienation, and estrangement. Thus in our study, amount of drug use was associated with low scores on the Social Responsibility factor ($r = -0.19$); and in girls with a sense of alienation ($r = 0.30$ with a project-constructed measure of alienation) and an external locus of control ($r = -0.33$ with the Nowicki-Strickland [1973] [internal] Locus of Control measure).

Although the short-range effects of euphoria-producing drugs are to enhance self-esteem the long-range effects are likely to be in the opposite direction. The self-enhancing effects of taking drugs are a result of the euphoric mood experienced and of the sense of acceptance provided by cult support. By foreclosing options for ego enhancement based on achievement and competence, drug-using adolescents may fail to acquire those skills required for a realistic sense of control over the environment. Habits

of work and values internalized in childhood may be suppressed or sub-
verted as a result of the dramatic alterations in mental functioning induced
by psychedelic drugs and marijuana, further aggravating the generational
rift. Parents may then feel obliged either to reinstate age-inappropriate
controls or to reject the defiant adolescent altogether. To the extent that
members of mainstream reference groups continue to be important to
drug-using youths, their disapprobation will negatively affect these youths'
self-concept directly as well as indirectly by foreclosing employment and
scholastic options these mainstream members control.

The Impact of Social Policy on Adolescent Alienation and Commitment

Social policy and intervention strategies over the past twenty years
have not rectified conditions that contribute to adolescent alienation.
Indeed, by eroding the ecology of family and school life, social experiments in the last two decades may have contributed more to the problem
of adolescent alienation than to its resolution (Baumrind, 1974, 1975,
1978a, 1978b; Bronfenbrenner, 1979; Moynihan, 1986). The common thread
running through the commission reports and conferences on youth in the
1970s was that the powerlessness of young people should be redressed by
increasing their rights and privileges and by decreasing the negative sanc-
tions and lowering the standards applied to their behavior in school and
family contexts. These presuppositions reflected an unexamined liberal
ideology that grouped youth with disenfranchised minorities as victims of
society. The rhetoric of the children's rights movement contained for example in the Coleman II report referred to youth as a "subordinate nation"
(Coleman, 1974), comparing their position to that of blacks. The defiant
Bill of Rights of the White House Conference on Youth (written 1971,
cited in Coleman, 1974, p. 23) proclaimed for youth "the right . . . to do
his/her thing, so long as it does not interfere with the rights of another"
and "the right to do whatever is necessary to preserve these rights." The
negative attitude of many adults toward themselves and their generation,
exemplified in the wave of mea culpa literature that appeared the 1960s
and 1970s (such as Friedenberg's *The Anti-American Generation*, 1971;
Osborne's *How to Deal With Parents and Other Problems*, 1962; and
Reich's *The Greening of America*, 1970) contributed to the malaise that
afflicted many adolescents during that period.

Social interventions from the 1960s to the present day have trans-
ferred the locus of control for adolescent problem behavior from the family
to other social institutions and tacitly, if not explicitly, have adopted a
value-neutral approach. For example, family planning clinics that serve
early adolescents do not require parental consent or knowledge. Educational programs are designed to impart objective information on such

loaded issues as adolescent sexuality and drug experimentation. However, such value-neutral programs may actually subvert the values of conservative parents and weaken their authority.

Knowing as we do that inaction by adults observing aggressive acts in young children increases the incidence of such antisocial behavior (see Siegel and Kohn, 1959; Spence, 1966), and more specifically, that drug information programs designed to increase knowledge also—and inadvertently—increase experimentation (see Stuart, 1974), we need to reassess the neutrality of the value-neutral stance. Although parent groups such as Toughlove, which are forming in reaction to a permissive social climate, are often overly authoritarian and therefore less effective than they might be, their concerns are legitimate. Value-neutral programs in the schools and family planning agencies that bypass parental consent should be reexamined with a view toward their possible effects on adolescents' ethical beliefs and on the attachment and disciplinary bonds between adolescents and their parents.

The Western emphasis on individualism at the expense of interdependence has shaped our presuppositions about the process of adolescent individuation. The concept of individualism presumes that each of us is an entity separate from the rest, separate of the autonomous self from the genealogical family and kinship group. But one's parents are literally a part of oneself, both genetically and as a result of the socialization process, and a self-concept that denies one's continuity with one's parents is bound to be problematic. Based on unproven early psychoanalytic presuppositions, it has been widely accepted that the process of adolescent individuation requires loosening of family ties and "infantile" objective attachments. Current psychoanalytic formulations (see Beiser, 1980; Blos, 1979; Coleman, 1978; Spotts and Shontz, 1985), while less dogmatic in placing blame for adolescent problems on "overprotective" mothers, still emphasize the need for emotional separation from parents as a precondition of adolescent individuation. The view that it is natural and desirable for adolescents to transfer emotional attachments from parents to peers is supported by Piaget's distinctions ([1932] 1965) between heteronomous and autonomous morality: A young child's heteronomous view of authority as unilateral and role bound is supplanted during adolescence by an autonomous view of authority arising from symmetrical and reciprocal relationships established among peers. It is presumed therefore that adolescents who remain emotionally attached to parents and respectful of their authority are immature.

None of these presuppositions has been systematically examined, and it may be that they are valid in clinical contexts but not in normal populations. The emphasis (or overemphasis) on individualism in the American ego ideal denies the objective reality that the boundaries separating self from nonself are permeable. Self is literally constructed in interaction with nonself. The exaggerated emphasis in the American character on personal freedom and autonomy, while contributing to our material prosperity and democratic traditions, also leaves us vulnerable to alienation. Alienation is a consequence of separating oneself from the physical and social environment in which one is naturally embedded, whereas commitment follows from a conception of nature as one's own real body, of physical nature as one's organic flesh and of the social environment as one's inorganic flesh. The normal need at all ages for communion is peculiarly unmet during the early adolescent transition, because adolescents are seldom mature enough to establish mutually gratifying intimate relationships with peers and parents are warned against maintaining close emotional attachments with their adolescent children. Adolescents' normal yearning for communion and dissolution of boundaries may drive some into religious cults, some to promiscuous sex, and others to psychedelic drugs.

The implicit values and presuppositions of clinicians working within a psychoanalytical or Piagetian framework contrast sharply with those of contemporary researchers concerned with the prevention of adolescent drug abuse (such as Jessor and Jessor, 1977, 1978). For example, the developmental pattern that Jessor and Jessor (1978) refer to as "transition-proneness" and label as "deviant" is also descriptive of mature, healthy adolescents. This pattern, which admittedly describes the adolescent drug user, also includes most of the attitudes that characterize the typical advent of psychosocial adolescence, namely, higher value on independence; increased social criticism and political activism; decreased religiosity; increased perceived friends' support relative to parents' support; increased perceived relaxation of parents' standards; lowered reported church attendance; and increased reported drinking, social activism, alcohol use, drug use, and sexual activity. The two important exceptions to the nearly perfect correspondence between responses indicative of normal psychosocial development and transition-proneness is on lowered achievement motivation and sense of alienation: Jessor and Jessor reported developmental decreases in alienation from the freshman to the senior high school years but found that higher alienation predicts onset of marijuana use. Since alienation and lowered academic motivation do not contribute to healthy risk-taking behavior or optimum development, these are viably targeted behaviors for preventive-intervention programs, unlike the other transition-prone characteristics that are associated with social maturity for adolescents.

In opposition to the message of Freudian or Piagetian stage theorists, the implicit prescription of practitioners and researchers concerned with preventing adolescent deviance is to postpone psychosocial adolescence as long as possible in order to prevent risk-taking behavior. Retarding development is not a practical intervention strategy, although persuading healthy mature adolescents that drug use has harmful consequences might be, provided that we could document these harmful consequences as well as we have been able to do for smoking behavior. Deviance theorists are certainly correct in pointing out the negative consequences of premature adolescent emancipation from parent control.

The progressive weakening of the bond between parents and their adolescents over the last two decades has been adult rather than youth initiated. The reduction of legal adult status to age 18 under the guise of offering adolescents their freedom in effect liberated parents from their children. However, I note two recent themes in the thinking of health care professionals and developmental psychologists that could benefit the relationship between young people and their parents: (1) a renewed interest in the role of moral values in everyday life, and (2) a recognition of the importance of family attachments and supervision during the adolescent transition.

Moral Rejuvenation. Adolescents cannot be expected to accept uncritically the values of their elders. However, there is growing recognition that young people need to be presented with rationally justified, stable, coherent adult values against which to test their own emerging moral judgments. In the absence of firm adult guidelines, youths are forced to rely on the guidelines of the peer culture, which are necessarily immature and untested. However, it is essential in a pluralistic society that where adult values are imparted in the school setting they represent the consensus of parents in each local community. Jesse Jackson together with other black church leaders calls for moral rejuvenation. Jackson's mottoes, pertinent and unambiguous—hope not dope; babies should not have babies—represent the consensus of the black adult community.

Values about which there is consensus in most communities include the civic virtues of due process, majority rule, and civil liberties for the minority and the personal virtues of compassion, courage, tolerance, and fairness. National Opinion Research Center (NORC) figures for 1985, compared to those of 1980, show a conservative trend among youth as well as other segments of society (Davis and Smith, 1985). Today's young people, compared to their counterparts in the 1960s, do not favor promiscuous sex, abortion on demand, or legalization of all drug use. However, the values of the Moral Majority, as they mistakenly call themselves, represent the consensual values of few, if any, communities. The NORC surveys find that today's young people are more worldly and better educated than their elders were at their age and generally concerned with religion and do not, on the whole, accept the fundamentalist bans on extramarital sex and abortion. They do, however, favor premarital sex within a committed relationship. Especially because first marriage is taking place at a later age, responsible premarital sex delayed until late adolescence is a more rational health care objective than the bans on nonmarital sex by the Moral Majority. The alarming increase in sexually transmitted diseases, most notably herpes and AIDS, has had a deterrent impact on sexual promiscuity that may last.

Family Attachments and Supervision. A consensus appears to be developing among investigators concerned with adolescent welfare that engagement with, rather than separation from, parents during early adolescence enhances adolescents' ego development and individuation by reducing their susceptibility to peer pressure. Cooper, Grotevant, and Condon (1983), in their contribution to collection of essays on adolescent development in the family, described the effective family system as one that avoids both enmeshment, in which family members are expected to act and think alike, as well as disengagement, in which family members are so separate that they have little effect on each other. Family processes that balance expressions of individuality (both self-assertion and differentiation of self from others) with expressions of connectedness (permeability to and respect for the views of others) are most effective in generating competence. In the same vein, Steinberg (1985) presents data to support his claim that emotional distance from the family results in heightened susceptibility to peer influences. The data I presented earlier shows that drug use is positively related to desire to please peers and negatively related to desire to please adults. Similarly, contributors to a recent conference sponsored by the Office of Science of the National Institute on Drug Abuse (NIDA) (Hawkins, Lishner, and Catalano, 1985) proposed that youths are more susceptible to negative peer influences when the social bonds of attachment and commitment to prosocial others are weakened. They concluded that parents who use authoritative management skills, including effective and open communication, consistent support, and firm enforcement of mutually agreed on rules that respect the developmental needs of adolescents, are better able to prevent adolescent drug abuse than parents who are either more lenient or more restrictive.

In short, there is an emerging consensus that successful negotiation of the adolescent transition lies not in asserting independence for the purpose of overcoming the dependency of childhood but rather in establishing modes of interdependence through familial reorganization of rights, responsibilities, and personal relationships.

Traditional, Authoritarian-Restrictive, Punitive, and Authoritative Prototypes and Adult Authority

The impact on adolescents of nonlenient parental authority differs depending on the child-rearing context in which it is embedded. We may distinguish among four prototypic nonlenient patterns: (1) traditional, (2) authoritarian-restrictive, (3) punitive, and (4) authoritative. These patterns, together with others descriptive of lenient parenting, emerged from assessments of parents in my longitudinal study.

Traditional. Traditional families value a sense of continuity and order more than innovation and risk-taking. They accept the pattern of understanding and the value judgments that have been worked out over time by previous generations. Youths from homes in which both parents are religious and abstainers from alcohol are more likely to internalize an abstinence norm and refrain from drinking after making the transition from home to college environment (Campbell, 1964). Clausen (1966), in an analysis of Oakland Growth Study data, found that youths who demonstrated compliant dependence on their parents and whose parents did not smoke internalized the smoking prohibitions of their parents. In a preliminary study confirmed by more recent data, Baumrind (1971b) found that adolescents who claimed to never have used illicit drugs were more attached to their parents, more conforming, and more achievement oriented. However, they were somewhat less intelligent than adolescents who had experimented with drugs. Blum and Associates (1972) found that adolescent drug use was least prevalent among traditional families who both disciplined their children and spent much time with them and for whom religion played an ongoing part in family and community life.

Families who maintain a strong belief system and a traditional family structure seem best able to shield their children from drug use and anomie. Middle-class youths who remain encapsulated within a traditional family structure in a traditional community may circumvent altogether the adolescent individuation crisis and the problem behaviors that often accompany it as may lower-class youths whose lives are made real by the struggle to survive. However, there is a price to be paid for bypassing the individuation crisis. These young people are likely to show deficits in the areas of autonomy and creativity.

Authoritarian-Restrictive. Traditional parents are not necessarily authoritarian. In traditional homes the father exercises authority firmly early in the child's life so that the child may develop the self-discipline that permits independence later on. By contrast, authoritarian parents believe in keeping children, even adolescents, in a subordinate role, in restricting their autonomy, and in not encouraging verbal interchange and negotiation. They do not willingly share power and responsibility even with their adolescents and in this sense violate the implicit contract in which parental authority is exercised to benefit primarily the child rather than the parent. A notion of contract is fundamental to the justice conception that develops during adolescence, particularly among educated middle-class youths. The making of contracts presupposes the liberty of the contractees. When coercive authority is not relinquished during the adolescent transition, children are less likely to attribute responsibility to themselves as moral agents (Lepper, 1981) and therefore not to feel obliged to abide by the explicit or implicit contracts they have with their parents or with society. Authoritarian parents, unlike traditional parents, are likely therefore to incite reactive rebellion in some adolescents as well as to reduce the moral maturity of most.

Punitive. Neither traditional nor authoritarian parents are necessarily punitive. Harsh parental treatment may convince the adolescent that morality is inevitably arbitrary and self-serving, thus providing a rationale in experience for immoral behavior. Harsh, punitive parental practices are associated with low expressions of guilt, an external orientation to transgressions, and antisocial aggression in children and adolescents. These findings hold equally for delinquent adolescent males (see Bandura and Walters, 1959; Glueck and Glueck, 1950; Hetherington, Stouwie, and Ridberg, 1971; McCord, McCord, and Zola, 1959; Wittman and Huffman, 1945), for delinquent adolescent females (Hetherington, Stouwie, and Ridberg, 1971; Wittman and Huffman, 1945), and for all ages and classes studied (Becker and others, 1959; Martin and Hetherington, 1971; McCord, McCord, and Howard, 1961; Winder and Rau, 1962).

Authoritative. Authoritative parents, by definition, are not punitive or authoritarian. They may however embrace traditional values. Authoritative parents, in comparison to lenient parents, are more demanding and, in comparison to authoritarian-restrictive parents, are more responsive. Authoritative parents are demanding in that they guide their children's activities firmly and consistently and require them to contribute to family functioning by helping with household tasks. They willingly confront their children in order to obtain conformity, state their values clearly, and expect their children to respect their norms. Authoritative parents are responsive affectively in the sense of being loving, supportive, and committed; they are responsive cognitively in the sense of providing a stimulating and challenging environment. Authoritative parents characteristically maintain an appropriate ratio of children's autonomy to parental control at all ages. However, an appropriate ratio is weighted in the direction of control with young children and in the direction of autonomy in adolescence. Authoritative parents of adolescents focus on issues rather than personalities and roles, they encourage their adolescents to voice their dissent and actively seek to share power as their children mature.

I have described the authoritative pattern of parental control and differentiated it from permissive-lenient and authoritarian-restrictive patterns in a series of articles published over the last twenty years (Baumrind, 1966, 1968, 1971a, 1975, 1978a, 1983, forthcoming). In three preschool samples and one primary school sample, I found that authoritative parental control was associated with outstanding instrumental competence. The primary school sample (time 2) is part of a longitudinal study in progress whose subjects were last seen during early adolescence (time 3). Preliminary analyses of the adolescent data indicate that adolescents whose parents were authoritative at time 2 remain competent at time 3.

In the preschool samples, authoritative parental behavior was associated with independent, purposive, dominant, and achievement-oriented behavior in girls. In boys, authoritative control was associated with social responsibility, cognitive competence, and somewhat above-average social assertiveness. Permissive and authoritarian parents differed in the nurturance-control ratio (with permissive parents higher in nurturance and authoritarian parents higher in control), but both lacked balance between what was offered to their children in the way of support and what was demanded of them in terms of obedience. True, the imbalance was in opposite directions, but it was difficult to distinguish between the effects of these two kinds of imbalance in the early years. Authoritative parents, by contrast, balanced what they demanded with what they offered: high control with high independence-granting, high standards for maturity with much support and nurturance. Both permissive and authoritarian parents differed significantly from authoritative parents in that they lacked confidence in their childrearing practices, did not enrich their children's environment, and, for boys, did not have a clearly defined childrearing policy.

In the primary school sample, the children of authoritative parents were distinguished from the children of other parent types in that they were more competent, excelling in non-sex-typed attributes: Daughters of parents who were authoritative in the primary school years were most socially assertive and significantly more so at both ages 9 and 14 than daughters of permissive parents; sons of parents who were authoritative in the primary school years were most socially responsible and significantly more so at age 9 and later at age 14 than sons of rejecting parents. Firm control and direct confrontation were the most important determinants of competence in girls whereas maternal responsiveness was a major determinant of competence in boys. When parents were detached or unengaged at age 9, even if they were not overtly rejecting, children of both sexes were incompetent, and boys at both ages 9 and 14 were lacking in social responsibility.

Data from the adolescent wave of this longitudinal study are in the first stage of analysis. Parents have not yet been grouped on the basis of their time 3 adolescent child-rearing practices. On the basis of theory and previous work, however, I expect to find a group of parents who, following puberty, engage their adolescents in an actively negotiated reorganization of family structure in which the asymmetrical assignment of power and obligations characteristic of childhood gives way to a more symmetrical distribution of rights and responsibilities. More specifically, these authoritative parents will negotiate standards and limits, sustain a strong bond of attachment with their adolescents, and use reasoning and example to legitimate their moral authority. Pikas (1961), in his survey of 656 Swedish adolescents, showed that parental authority that was based on rational concern for the adolescent welfare was regarded by adolescents as legitimate, while authority based on the adult's desire to dominate or exploit the child was rejected. The former, which Pikas calls rational authority, is similar to what I have designated authoritative control, and the latter, which he calls inhibiting authority, is similar to what I have designated authoritarian control. His results are supported by Middleton and Putney (1963), who found that parental discipline regarded by the child as either very strict or very permissive was associated with lack of closeness between parent and child and with rebellion against the parents' political viewpoints. Similarly, Elder (1963) found that junior and senior high school students were more likely to model themselves after their parents and to associate with parent-approved peers if their parents used reason to explain decisions and demands. However, when a permissive climate of upbringing predominates as it did in the late 1960s and 1970s or when one parent undermines the authority of the other, even authoritative control may be perceived by adolescents as restrictive and not accepted by them as legitimate.

The success of traditional families in shielding their children from dysfunctional risk-taking behavior appears to be less a consequence of their conservative values than of two factors that they share with less conservative parents: strong mutual attachments that persist through adolescence and coherent, consistent management policies. Although parents have not yet been grouped on the basis of their time 3 child-rearing behavior, early analyses reveal that adolescent boys whose parents were classified at time 2 as democratic (moderately controlling but highly responsive and autonomy granting) are rated by observers as socially assertive as well as socially responsible, and that adolescent girls whose parents were earlier classified as traditional are not rated as socially assertive. When the children were age 9, the positive effects of democratic upbringing on boys' social responsibility and assertiveness, and the negative effects of traditional upbringing on girls' social assertiveness, were not apparent. Parents who were classified as authoritative at time 2 have children who are socially responsible and assertive at both time 2 and time 3. Thus democratic or authoritative parents who, like traditional parents, are firm and committed but who in addition embrace nontraditional beliefs may also be able to shield their adolescents from dysfunctional risk-taking behavior, and they may be able to do so without the loss in social assertiveness and creativity that appears to occur in adolescent girls in traditional homes.

Funding Issues, Research Design, and Priority Areas

In this concluding section I will address some problems about research funding, recommend research strategies that may be more effective than those that have been favored by review groups, and propose that five broad research areas be given funding priority.

Research Funding: Problems and Recommendations. The fragmentation of funding among the various national institutes has contributed to a fragmented understanding of adolescent problem behaviors. Grouping these problem behaviors under a single rubric such as risk taking manifests a new and welcome recognition that adolescent pregnancy, drug abuse, smoking, alcohol abuse, automotive recklessness, delinquency, prostitution, and running away all are symptoms of a common malaise. Ideally a National Institute of Adolescent Health should be established to coordinate the research on adolescent health and dysfunction and to find ways of strengthening the family, school, and community as supportive institutions to prevent the manifestations of adolescent alienation. Interagency requests for proposals (RFPs), provided that they are backed up by adequate funding, would also be helpful. (The three institutes of the Alcohol, Drug Abuse, and Mental Health Administration [ADAMHA] jointly released a grant announcement in August 1983 inviting methodologically rigorous applications using existing longitudinal data to improve our understanding of known risk factors and precursors of alcohol abuse, drug abuse, and mental illness in children and adolescents. But, unfortunately, the total availability of funds for these new awards to be spread over the fiscal years of 1984 and 1985 was a token $500,000!)

Changes are required in the peer review system to circumvent the nearly unanimous vote of confidence needed to obtain a priority score that is high enough to guarantee funding. The necessity for unanimity caters to cronyism and excessively conservative research designs, penalizing innovative researchers.

In addition, a mechanism should be found to provide long-term support for the research efforts of investigators engaged in longitudinal studies. Research career awards are of great help to seasoned investigators of proven worth, but the work of such investigators can be seriously hampered by the waste of time and energy necessitated by incessant submission of grant applications to support research efforts.

Research Design Issues. In the past decade, social-behavioral studies of drug abuse have been dominated by the social-survey methods favored by epidemiologists. As a result, the natural history of the phenomenon of adolescent substance abuse over that period of time has been well documented. However, this body of research suffers from deficiencies inherent in the use of extensive social-survey methods to assess a phenomenon that requires intensive intraindividual assessments within a longitudinal design. There is still a need for further information about why early adolescents use drugs; how the family, school, and other social institutions could prevent drug use; and what strategies might intervene to prevent drug experimenters from becoming drug abusers. More attention needs to be paid to the individual and stage-related characteristics of the user, to the process of becoming a drug user, and to the drug-using experience itself. In order to obtain more relevant and reliable knowledge about the causes and prevention of such maladaptive coping strategies as drug abuse by adolescents, I recommend that we depart from the epidemiological model and from associated data-collection strategies restricted to questionnaires and brief structured interviews. In order to investigate the five priority areas described in the following section, I have the following recommendations:

1. Intensive, multidimensional, multisituational assessments of individuals are required to provide ecologically valid data relevant to the clinical concerns of therapists and health care practitioners. Earlier work in the field (Becker, 1963; Blum and Associates, 1972; Keniston, 1965) featured just such in-depth, comprehensive analyses of the drug-using experience, using small samples with variables embedded within a theoretical context. However, the data-analytic methods used by these investigators were deficient by today's standards: The sophisticated multivariate statistics and computer programs that we take for granted today were not then available. Moreover, reports were embedded in an understanding of pathological rather than normal development or generalized from knowledge of very heavy users to the experience of moderate, regular users (Hendin and others, 1981). Today, however, the tail wags the dog: Powerful data-analytic strategies frequently substitute for systematic theory and articulate hypothetical constructs, and data quality is sacrificed to obtain the large samples required by the multivariate analyses.

2. Fiscal constraints place a limit on the number of subjects that can be studied intensively. Medium-size samples of 150 are large enough for quantitative analyses and small enough for intensive assessment of each case provided that (1) the sample is homogeneous with regard to such background factors as age, SES, and ethnicity; and (2) trained professionals are used to make assessments.

3. Samples should be drawn from a variety of populations, each selected because of the kinds of problem youths it contains. The causes, consequences, and natural history of manifestations of alienation among upper-middle-class youths in a college town such as Berkeley, California, will differ in important ways from the same phenomenon observed among youths in a Chicago ghetto. Results may be specific to the particular population from which the sample is drawn, but converging generalizations are likely to emerge that apply across several social contexts. In order to achieve an in-depth understanding of the phenomenon of adolescent alienation, it is a better strategy to collect a representative sample of behavior from a homogeneous sample of subjects than to collect an unrepresentative sample of behavior from a heterogeneous group of subjects that is presumed to represent the American people as a whole.

4. The whole person should be the unit of study and adolescent problem behavior and pathology understood in the context of contemporary youth culture and normal development. Prototypic cases can be selected from the larger sample to provide qualitative information. With a

sample size of 150 and the use of factor analytic methods, the identification of theoretically relevant life-styles and prototypic cases can be made objectively after the basic data on subjects in the larger sample have been examined using standard quantitative dimensional analyses. In this way the uniqueness of personal, psychological life-styles can be taken into account and described. But in contrast to the representative case method of Spotts and Shontz (1985), the life-styles themselves can be identified by objective quantitative methods.

5. Short-term longitudinal studies in which subjects are studied before, during, and after the adolescent transition are needed to identify types of adolescents with contrasting patterns of risk-taking behavior. Cross-sectional studies cannot assess the differential developmental paths taken from midchildhood through the adolescent transition by types of youth whose life-styles differ with regard to the degree of alienation they experience and the troublesome symptoms of alienation they manifest. Behavior that in the short-run poses an objective risk to mortality or morbidity, as for example militant political involvement or mountain climbing, may in the long-run benefit the individual or the community. On the other hand, the objective risk factor of a particular form of behavior such as habitual marijuana use may become apparent only by observing how its long-range consequences alter the developmental trajectory of the individual. Thus among adolescent marijuana users, our longitudinal data document the presence of a cognitive deficit reflecting an amotivational syndrome that was not present at age 9 prior to drug use, that is not present in adolescents who do not use any drugs recreationally, and is not as strongly present in adolescents who use alcohol but not marijuana.

Priority Areas for Research. I have selected five priority areas in which data are needed to inform prevention and intervention programs. Additional priority areas will doubtless be nominated by other authors.

Family Reorganization in the Adolescent Transition. The adolescent transition can be thought of also as a family transition. There are relatively few studies that focus on the important role of the family in facilitating secure passage during the adolescent's transition from the status of a child to that of an adult. The conceptions of parents as well as investigators differ about how to define normal adolescent individuation and what kind of family reorganization, if any, is needed to achieve it. Can families be differentiated on the basis of their own implicit or explicit model of how, or if, the family should be restructured during adolescence: for example, that family structure during adolescence should (1) remain asymmetrical as in childhood, (2) move toward mutual separation and independence, or (3) move toward symmetrical interdependence? What impact does the model adopted have on adolescent competence and problem behavior? Are expressions of defiance, provocation, and self-destructiveness such as drug abuse more likely to be fostered by parents' reluctance to let go as conventional wisdom dictates, or by parents' failure to sustain a climate of control and commitment as I have suggested here?

Alternatives to the Nuclear Family. Even the nuclear family with both parents working has difficulty sustaining strong kinship bonds and adequate supervision of adolescents. However, the traditional nuclear family is no longer normative throughout the adolescent transition. Single mothers, as well as stepparent families, appear to have special problems legitimating their authority during adolescence. Newly emerging alternatives include gay and lesbian families; older, affluent single mothers who choose never to marry; and multiple "parent" families. We have little or no information on the course of development or extent of morbidity and mortality among the adolescent offspring of these relationships. Do any of these alternatives to the nuclear family provide the sustained commitment and supervision adolescents appear to need?

Adolescent Values and Moral Orientation. Three kinds of studies in the moral domain are of interest:

1. Needed are large-sample questionnaire data supplemented by data obtained from intensive interviews with a selected representative sample that document adolescents' actual values and moral orientation and relate these values to the adolescents' upbringing and subsequent behavior. To what extent do the beliefs and values of young people determine their risk-taking behavior? Do strong beliefs and clear moral standards provide countervailing influences to adverse social conditions and enable some individuals to flourish despite such social conditions? Are some adolescents no longer ashamed of becoming pregnant and going on welfare? Are macho values associated with destructive risk-taking behavior? Is there evidence that, as Yankelovich (1981) suggests, more youths are embracing an ethic of commitment rather than one either of self-denial or self-gratification? How do adolescents evaluate the dangers to themselves of the activities we group under the risk-taking rubric? Do adolescents typically differentiate between risks they can control and that can result in mastery and dangers they cannot or choose not to control and that do not lead to mastery? If so, do they place a positive value on the former and a negative value on the latter, or do they value all alike as good or bad? What are the socialization antecedents and the consequences for adolescents' health of their values and moral orientations?

2. Studies that test the effect of value-neutral versus evaluative programs for youth are needed. The climate of opinion has turned away from the value-clarification approach, with its moral neutrality, to a value-education approach that seeks to teach and inculcate values about which there is social consensus. For example, at the urging of parents, the Fresno Unified School District has developed a value-education curriculum beginning in the fourth grade that directly teaches the consensual civic and personal values held by Fresno parents. What is the impact on adolescents'

values and risk-taking behaviors of such programs or for example of those proposed by Jesse Jackson for the black community as compared to the effects of neutral value-clarification programs?

3. Studies are needed that redefine alienation for contemporary youth. What is the extent and expression of alienation among today's youth? Is there a relation between diminished expectations for traditional material rewards and a sense of alienation? What are the commitments, if any, of inner-city youths who do not expect to share in the American Dream no matter how hard they work? Do middle-class youths continue to value these traditional rewards and believe that if they work hard enough they can earn them?

Adolescents' Conceptions of Risk. The norms of adolescent behavior, and possibly their conceptions of risk, have changed historically in response to the earlier age at which puberty is reached and to the rapidly changing risk factors in the social environment. What do activities that adults define as dangerous accomplish *for* adolescents from their own perspective? We have an excellent opportunity to study adolescents' changing conceptions of risk-taking about a valued activity that has been clearly identified as dangerous by focusing attention on the sexual attitudes and activities of young gay men confronted with the known danger of AIDS.

Willingness to take personal risks for the sake of development is a mark of maturity in adulthood. Some risk-taking activities may be valued by adolescents because they are thought to prepare them to assume adult status. When an activity is associated with emancipated or adult status as, for example, smoking is for young women, is it still possible to create a moral climate that opposes it? The creation of a moral climate opposed to smoking has been an effective deterrent for young men but less so for young women, who continue to associate smoking with emancipation. Prevention and intervention programs can be most effective when they take into account adolescents' own beliefs and values. These are often at variance with those of social policy planners and health professionals. If, from the perspective of black youths, sex and parenthood confer status and a sense of belonging and if being supported by welfare has become more acceptable morally to teenage mothers, then a different prevention strategy is needed than if the increase in children born to black teens is due primarily to the unavailability of contraceptives or to ignorance about how to use them.

The Identification of Childhood Risk Factors Associated with Positive and Negative Adolescent Outcomes. The problems adolescents present generally have their origins in childhood patterns or socialization experiences. Children at risk for engaging in dysfunctional risk-taking behavior in adolescence need to be identified early. For example, children who suffer from attention deficit disorder with hyperactivity have greater difficulty than normal children in successfully accomplishing the tasks of adolescence

(Raskin, 1985). Such children do not intentionally seek stress but unwittingly become involved in activities that are dangerous. Adopted children, especially sons, in single-parent families may be especially at risk. In our longitudinal study, of the sixteen family units in which the father had left home before the target child was age ten, eleven contained daughters of whom only one was adopted (she is the only adopted girl in the study) and five contained sons all of whom were adopted. Of these five boys, four were seriously disturbed by adolescence, as was the one girl. The one adopted boy whose parents did not divorce remained healthy. No father of a natural son left the home early, whereas ten fathers of natural daughters did. The coincidence of adoptive status of sons and father absence may be a peculiarity of our sample. It is possible however that fathers feel a strong bond of attachment and commitment to their natural sons that they do not share with their adopted sons. If so, adopted boys are at special risk during the adolescent period. In order to trace the developmental sequencing among the risk factors (as for example adoptive status) for maladaptive adolescent coping behavior, prospective longitudinal research with measurement repeated at frequent intervals throughout childhood and into early adulthood is needed. At a minimum, four time periods—middle childhood, early adolescence, late adolescence, and early adulthood—are required to document the changes that take place during the adolescent transition. Adolescent activities that have contributed to unfavorable outcomes in early adulthood can be designated as problematic and the antecedents in early and middle childhood of such activities identified.

Conclusion

In conclusion, I want to summarize my major assertions that, although they have some research support, should not be regarded as proven premises but rather as a framework for generating hypotheses to be tested through basic research and intervention experiments. I have asserted that it is important to distinguish between normal transitional risk-taking behavior and pathological or pathogenic expressions for which secondary gains are virtually absent. The many forms of destructive behavior we label risk-taking are symptoms of a sense of alienation. Risk taking becomes destructive when it contributes directly or indirectly to the process of becoming alienated rather than to exploratory and experimental processes that are developmentally normal and preparatory to commitment. I have also asserted that it is the task of adult leaders, including parents, to educate young people in the collective traditions of their society and in the civic and personal virtues they incorporate, rather than to present these traditions in a value-neutral context. It is the task of each generation to reevaluate traditions passed on by the previous generations. Unreflective acceptance of these traditions produces clones with foreclosed identities.

Unreflective rejection of these traditions leaves adolescents vulnerable to alienation. Adolescents are best able to reflect on these traditions when adults present their own values clearly but just as clearly encourage adolescents to examine and critique them. I have proposed that adolescents are more competent and morally developed when they function interdependently, not independently. The major task of the adolescent period of development, therefore, is movement away from dependence on the family, not toward independence but rather toward interdependence. I have claimed that individuation does not require adolescents to emotionally distance themselves from parents but rather for a reorganization to be undertaken in which family members renegotiate and redistribute entitlements and obligations. Finally, I have asserted that adolescent individuation is achieved not merely by an internal process of moral or cognitive development but rather by an active, if tentative, commitment to a calling, to friends, and to moral ideals.

References

Bachman, J. G., Green, S., and Wirtanen, I. "Dropping Out—Problem or Symptom?" *Youth in Transition*, 1971, *3*, 67–258.

Bandura, A., and Walters, L. H. *Adolescent Aggression: A Study of the Influences of Child-Training Practices and Family Interrelations.* New York: Ronald Press, 1959.

Baumrind, D. "Effects of Authoritative Parental Control on Child Behavior." *Child Development*, 1966, *37* (4), 887–907.

Baumrind, D. "Authoritarian Versus Authoritative Parental Control." *Adolescence*, 1968, *3* (2), 255–272.

Baumrind, D. "Current Patterns of Parental Authority." *Developmental Psychology Monograph*, 1971a, *4* (1, pt. 2), 1–103.

Baumrind, D. "Types of Adolescent Life-Styles." Unpublished manuscript, University of California, Berkeley, 1971b.

Baumrind, D. "Coleman II: Admixture of Utopian Fantasy and Sound Social Innovation." *School Review*, 1974, *82* (1), 69–84.

Baumrind, D. "Early Socialization and Adolescent Competence." In S. E. Dragastin and G. Elder, Jr. (eds.), *Adolescence in the Life Cycle.* Washington, D.C.: Hemisphere, 1975.

Baumrind, D. "Parental Disciplinary Patterns and Social Competence in Children." *Youth and Society*, 1978a, *9* (3), 239–276.

Baumrind, D. "Reciprocal Rights and Responsibilities in Parent-Child Relations." *Journal of Social Issues*, 1978b, *34* (2), 179–196.

Baumrind, D. "Rejoinder to Lewis's Reinterpretation of Parental Firm Control Effects: Are Authoritative Families Really Harmonious?" *Psychological Bulletin*, 1983, *94* (1), 132–144.

Baumrind, D. "Familial Antecedents of Adolescent Drug Use: A Developmental Perspective." In C. L. Jones and R. J. Battjes (eds.), *Etiology of Drug Abuse: Implications for Prevention.* NIDA Research Monograph no. 56. Rockville, Md.: National Institute on Drug Abuse, 1985.

Baumrind, D. *Familial Antecedents of Social Competence in Middle Childhood*, forthcoming.

122

Baumrind, D., and Moselle, K. "A Developmental Perspective on Adolescent Drug Abuse." *Advances in Alcohol and Substance Abuse*, 1985, *4* (3 and 4), 41–67.

Becker, H. S. *Outsiders: Studies in the Sociology of Deviance*. New York: Free Press, 1963.

Becker, W. C., Peterson, D. R., Hellmer, L. A., Shoemaker, D. J., and Quay, H. C. "Factors in Parental Behavior and Personality as Related to Problem Behavior in Children." *Journal of Consulting Psychology*, 1959, *23*, 107–118.

Beiser, H. R. "Ages 11 to 14." In S. Greenspan and G. Pollock (eds.), *The Course of Life: Psychoanalytic Contributions Toward Understanding Personality Development*. Vol. 2. *Latency, Adolescence and Youth*. Washington, D.C.: Government Printing Office, 1980.

Bellah, R. N., Madsen, R., Sullivan, W. M., Swidler, A., and Tipton, S. M. *Habits of the Heart: Individualism and Commitment in American Life*. Berkeley: University of California Press, 1985.

Blos, P. "The Second Individuation Process." In P. Blos (ed.), *The Adolescent Passage*. New York: International University Press, 1979.

Blum, R. H., and Associates. *Horatio Alger's Children: The Role of the Family in the Origin and Prevention of Drug Risk*. San Francisco: Jossey-Bass, 1972.

Brittain, C. V. "A Comparison of Urban and Rural Adolescence with Respect to Peer Versus Parent Compliance." *Adolescence*, 1968, *2*, 445–458.

Bronfenbrenner, U. *Two Worlds of Childhood: U.S. and U.S.S.R.* New York: Russell Sage, 1970.

Bronfenbrenner, U. *Influences on Human Development*. Hinsdale, Ill.: Dryden Press, 1972.

Bronfenbrenner, U. *The Ecology of Human Development: Experiments by Nature and Design*. Cambridge: Mass.: Harvard University Press, 1979.

Brown, B. F. *The Reform of Secondary Education: A Report to the Public and the Profession*. National Commission on the Reform of Secondary Education. New York: McGraw-Hill, 1973.

Campbell, E. Q. "The Internalization of Moral Norms." *Sociometry*, 1964, *27*, 391–412.

Clausen, J. A. "Family Structure, Socialization, and Personality." In L. W. Hoffman, and M. L. Hoffman (eds.), *Review of Child Development Research*. Vol. 2. New York: Russell Sage, 1966.

Coleman, J. S., (ed.). *Youth: Transition to Adulthood*. Report of the Panel on Youth of the President's Science Advisory Committee. Chicago: University of Chicago Press, 1974.

Coleman, J. S. "Current Contradictions in Adolescent Theory." *Journal of Youth and Adolescence*, 1978, *7*, 1–11.

Cooper, C. R., Grotevant, H. D., and Condon, S. M. "Individuality and Connectedness in the Family as a Context for Adolescent Identity Formation and Role-Taking Skill." In H. D. Grotevant and C. R. Cooper (eds.), *Adolescent Development in the Family*. New Directions for Child Development, no. 22. San Francisco: Jossey-Bass, 1983.

Crandall, V., Crandall, V. J., and Katkovsky, W. "A Children's Social Desirability Questionnaire." *Journal of Consulting Psychology*, 1965, *29*, 27–36.

Davis, J. A., and Smith, T. W. *General Social Survey 1972–1985*. Chicago: National Opinion Research Center, 1985.

Douvan, E., and Adelson, J. *The Adolescent Experience*. New York: Wiley, 1966.

Dubin, E. R., and Dubin, R. "The Authority Inception Period in Socialization." *Child Development*, 1963, *34*, 885–898.

Elder, G. H., Jr. "Parental Power Legitimation and Its Effect on the Adolescent." *Sociometry*, 1963, *25*, 50–65.

Elkind, D. "Egocentrism in Adolescence." *Child Development*, 1967, *38*, 1025–1034.

Erikson, E. H. "Identity and the Life Cycle: Selected Papers." *Psychological Issues*, 1959, *1* (1), 1–171.

Erikson, E. H. *Identity: Youth and Crisis.* New York: Norton, 1968.

Friedenberg, E. Z. (ed.). *The Anti-American Generation.* New Brunswick, N.J.: Transaction, 1971.

Gilligan, C. *In a Different Voice: Psychological Theory and Women's Development.* Cambridge, Mass.: Harvard University Press, 1982.

Glueck, S., and Glueck, E. *Unraveling Juvenile Delinquency.* New York: Commonwealth Fund, 1950.

Gordon, C. *Looking Ahead: Self-Conceptions, Race, and Family as Determinants of Adolescent Orientation to Achievement.* Washington, D.C.: American Sociological Association, 1972.

Hawkins, J. D., Lishner, D. M., and Catalano, R. F., Jr. "Childhood Predictors and the Prevention of Adolescent Substance Abuse." In C. L. Jones and R. J. Battjes (eds.), *Etiology of Drug Abuse: Implications for Prevention.* NIDA Research Monograph no. 56. Rockville, Md.: National Institute on Drug Abuse, 1985.

Hendin, H., Pollinger, A., Ulman, R., and Carr, A. C. *Adolescent Marijuana Abusers and Their Families.* National Institute on Drug Abuse Research Monograph no. 40. Washington, D.C.: U.S. Government Printing Office, 1981.

Hetherington, E. M., Stouwie, R. J., and Ridberg, E. H. "Patterns of Family Interaction and Child-Rearing Attitudes Related to Three Dimensions of Juvenile Delinquency." *Journal of Abnormal Psychology*, 1971, *78*, 160–176.

Heyneman, S. P. *Adolescence Research Opinion and National Youth Policy: What We Know and What We Don't Know.* Washington, D.C.: Social Research Group, George Washington University, 1976a.

Heyneman, S. P. "Continuing Issues in Adolescence: A Summary of Current Transition to Adulthood Debates." *Journal of Youth and Adolescence*, 1976b, *5* (4), 309–323.

Jessor, R., and Jessor, S. L. *Problem Behavior and Psychological Development: A Longitudinal Study of Youth.* Orlando, Fla.: Academic Press, 1977.

Jessor, R., and Jessor, S. L. "Theory Testing in Longitudinal Research on Marijuana Use." In D. B. Kandel (ed.), *Longitudinal Research on Drug Use: Empirical Findings and Methodological Issues.* Washington, D.C.: Hemisphere, 1978.

Jessor, S. L., and Jessor, R. "Maternal Ideology and Adolescent Problem Behavior." *Developmental Psychology*, 1974, *10*, 246–254.

Jorgenson, E. C., and Howell, R. J. "Changes in Self, Ideal-Self Correlations from Ages 3 Through 18." *Journal of Social Psychology*, 1969, *79*, 63–67.

Kandel, D. B., Kessler, R. C., and Margulies, R. Z. "Antecedents of Adolescent Initiation into Stages of Drug Use: A Developmental Analysis." In D. B. Kandel (ed.), *Longitudinal Research on Drug Use: Empirical Findings and Methodological Issues.* Washington, D.C.: Hemisphere, 1978.

Keniston, K. *The Uncommitted: Alienated Youth in America.* New York: Dell, 1965.

Kessen, W. (ed.). *Childhood in China.* New Haven: Yale University Press, 1975.

Kohlberg, L., and Gilligan, C. "The Adolescent as a Philosopher: The Discovery of the Self in a Post-Conventional World." In J. Kagan and R. Coles (eds.), *Twelve to Sixteen: Early Adolescence.* New York: Norton, 1972.

Langner, T. S., Gersten, J. C., Wills, T. A., and Simcha-Fagan, O. "The Relative Roles of Early Environment and Early Behavior as Predictors of Later Child

Behavior." In D. F. Ricks and B. S. Dohrenwend (eds.), *Origins of Psychopathology*. Cambridge, Mass.: Cambridge University Press, 1983.

Lenz, E., and Myerhoff, B. *The Feminization of America*. New York: Jeremy P. Tarcher, 1985.

Lepper, M. "Intrinsic and Extrinsic Motivation in Children: Detrimental Effects of Superfluous Social Controls." In W. A. Collins (ed.), *Aspects of the Development of Competence: The Minnesota Symposium on Child Psychology*. Vol. 14. Hillsdale, N.J.: Erlbaum, 1981.

McCord, W., McCord, J., and Howard, A. "Familial Correlates of Aggression in Nondelinquent Male Children." *Journal of Abnormal and Social Psychology*, 1961, *62*, 79-93.

McCord, W., McCord, J., and Zola, I. K. *Origins of Crime*. New York: Columbia University Press, 1959.

Martin, B., and Hetherington, E. M. *Family Interaction and Aggression, Withdrawal, and Nondeviancy in Children*. Bethesda, Md.: National Institute of Mental Health, 1971.

Marx, K. *Economic and Philosophic Manuscripts of 1844: Paris Manuscripts*. New York: International Publishers, 1964. (Originally published 1844.)

Marx, K. *Grundrisse*. D. McLellan (ed. and trans.). New York: Harper & Row, 1971. (Originally published 1858.)

Middleton, R., and Putney, S. "Political Expression of Adolescent Rebellion." *American Journal of Sociology*, 1963, *68*, 527-535.

Moynihan, D. P. *Family and Nation*. San Diego, Calif.: Harcourt Brace Jovanovich, 1986.

National Panel on High School and Adolescent Education. *The Education of Adolescents: Final Report and Recommendations*. Washington, D.C.: U.S. Office of Education, 1976.

Nickols, J. E., Jr. "Changes in Self-Awareness During the High School Years: A Study of Mental Health Using Paper-and-Pencil Tests." *Journal of Educational Research*, 1963, *56*, 403-409.

Nowicki, S., and Strickland, B. R. "A Locus of Control Scale for Children." *Journal of Consulting and Clinical Psychology*, 1973, *40*, 146-152.

Osborne, E. G. *How to Deal with Parents and Other Problems*. New York: Grosset & Dunlap, 1962.

Piaget, J. *Moral Judgment of the Child*. New York: Free Press, 1965. (Originally published 1932.)

Pikas, A. "Children's Attitudes Toward Rational Versus Inhibiting Parental Authority." *Journal of Abnormal Social Psychology*, 1961, *62*, 315-321.

Powers, S. I., Hauser, S. T., Schwartz, J. M., Noam, G. G., and Jacobson, A. M. "Adolescent Ego Development and Family Interaction: A Structural-Developmental Perspective." In H. D. Grotevant and C. R. Cooper (eds.), *Adolescent Development in the Family*. San Francisco: Jossey-Bass, 1983.

Raskin, A. (ed.). "Pharmacotherapy for ADD-H Adolescents Workshop." *Psychopharmacology Bulletin*, 1985, *21* (2), 167-258.

Reich, C. *The Greening of America*. New York: Random House, 1970.

Selman, R. "Taking Another's Perspective: Role-Taking Development in Early Childhood." *Child Development*, 1971, *42*, 79-91.

Selman, R. *The Growth of Interpersonal Understanding: Developmental and Clinical Analyses*. New York: Academic Press, 1980.

Siegel, A. E., and Kohn, L. G. "Permissiveness, Permission, and Aggression: The Effects of Adult Presence or Absence on Aggression in Children's Play." *Child Development*, 1959, *36*, 131-141.

Spence, J. T. "Verbal-Discrimination Performance as a Function of Instruction and Verbal Reinforcement Combination in Normal and Retarded Children." *Child Development,* 1966, *37,* 269-281.

Spotts, J. V., and Shontz, F. C. "A Theory of Adolescent Substance Abuse." *Advances in Alcohol and Substance Abuse,* 1985, *4* (3 and 4), 117-138.

Steinberg, L. *Adolescence.* New York: Knopf, 1985.

Stuart, R. "Teaching Facts About Drugs: Pushing or Preventing?" *Journal of Educational Psychology,* 1974, *66* (2), 189-201.

Timpane, M., Abramowitz, S., Bobrow, S., and Pascal, A. *Youth Policy in Transition.* Santa Monica, Calif.: Rand, 1976.

Turiel, E. "Social Regulations and Domains of Social Concepts." In W. Damon (ed.), *Social Cognition.* New Directions for Child Development, no. 1. San Francisco: Jossey-Bass, 1978.

Winder, C. L., and Rau, L. "Parental Attitudes Associated with Social Deviance in Preadolescent Boys." *Journal of Abnormal and Social Psychology,* 1962, *64,* 418-424.

Wittman, M. P., and Huffman, A. V. "A Comparative Study of Developmental Adjustment and Personality Characteristics of Psychotics, Psychoneurotics, Delinquent, and Normally Adjusted Teenaged Youths." *Journal of Genetic Psychology,* 1945, *66,* 167-182.

Wright, B. D. (ed.). *School Review,* 1974, *83* (1), entire issue.

Yamamoto, K., Thomas, E. C., and Karnes, E. A. "School-Related Attitudes in Middle-School Age Students." *American Educational Research Journal,* 1969, *6,* 191-206.

Yankelovich, D. *New Rules: Searching for Self-Fulfillment in a World Turned Upside Down.* New York: Random House, 1981.

Further Sources

Coleman, J. S. *The Adolescent Society.* New York: Free Press, 1961.

Elkind, D. "Middle-Class Delinquency." *Mental Health,* 1967, *5* (1), 80-84.

Hendin, H., and Haas, A. P. "The Adaptive Significance of Chronic Marijuana Use for Adolescents and Adults." *Advances in Alcohol and Substance Abuse,* 1985, *4* (3 and 4).

Jones, B. "The Dynamics of Marriage and Motherhood." In R. Morgan (ed.), *Sisterhood Is Powerful.* New York: Vintage, 1970.

Kaplan, H. B. *Deviant Behavior in Defense of Self.* New York: Academic Press, 1980.

Lasch, C. *The Culture of Narcissism: American Life in an Age of Diminishing Expectations.* New York: Norton, 1979.

Millett, K. *Sexual Politics.* New York: Doubleday, 1969.

Radl, S. *Mother's Day Is Over.* New York: McKay, 1973.

White House Conference on Youth. *Preamble: Recommendations and Resolutions.* Washington, D.C.: U.S. Government Printing Office, 1971.

Diana Baumrind is research psychologist at the Institute of Human Development at the University of California, Berkeley, and director of the Family Socialization and Developmental Competence Project—a longitudinal program of research. Her main research interest is parents' contribution to developmental competence and dysfunctional behavior throughout childhood and adolescence.

Index